Paragraph

T0386720

A Journal of Modern Critical Theory

Volume 34, Number 3, November 2011

Wittgenstein, Theory, Literature

Edited by James Helgeson

Contents

Introduction
JAMES HELGESON   287

Wittgenstein, von Wright and the Myth of Progress
JACQUES BOUVERESSE   301

Pierre Hadot as a Reader of Wittgenstein
SANDRA LAUGIER   322

What Cannot Be Said: Notes on Early French Wittgenstein
Reception
JAMES HELGESON   338

At the Margins of Sense: The Function of Paradox in Deleuze
and Wittgenstein
REIDAR A. DUE   358

Skinner, Wittgenstein and Historical Method
JONATHAN HAVERCROFT   371

Wittgenstein's *Philosophical Investigations*, Linguistic Meaning
and Music
GARRY L. HAGBERG   388

The Surrealism of the Habitual: From Poetic Language to the
Prose of Life
ALISON JAMES   406

Wittgenstein in Recent French Poetics: Henri Meschonnic and
Jacques Roubaud
MARIA RUSANDA MURESAN   423

Notes on Contributors   441

Index: *Paragraph* 34 (2011)   443

Paragraph is indexed in the Arts & Humanities Citation Index and
Current Contents/Arts & Humanities

Introduction

JAMES HELGESON

In a collection of filmed interviews from 1988 (first broadcast in 1996), *L'Abécédaire de Gilles Deleuze*, the French philosopher did not mince words about his antipathy for Ludwig Wittgenstein and his philosophical admirers. In the series, organized in the form of an alphabet-book ('W' for Wittgenstein), Deleuze's words are remarkable in their rhetorical violence:

I do not want to talk about that. For me, it's a philosophical catastrophe, a (...) massive step backwards for all of philosophy. It's very sad, the Wittgenstein business. They have put into place a system of terror under the pretext of saying something new. (...) It is poverty set up as grandeur. There is no word to describe that danger (...)

It's serious, above all because the Wittgenstinians are mean-spirited, and they destroy everything. If they win, philosophy will be assassinated — if they win. They are murderers of philosophy. It is necessary to be very vigilant.[1]

Such a forceful rejection must be understood in context. The history of Wittgenstein reception in France has been a complicated one, and Deleuze's reaction, although extreme, reflects the relative rarity of engagement with Wittgenstein among Deleuze's contemporaries and interlocutors. In the last twenty-five years, by contrast, there has been an explosion of interest in Wittgenstein in France, and it is perhaps already to the intimation of this change in fortune that Deleuze is reacting in the interview.[2]

This special issue does not attempt to reintroduce the philosopher into a critical debate in the humanities from which he cannot be said to have been absent. Rather, it aims to look at the diverse ways Wittgenstein can serve today as a point of reference for interpretation within the humanities broadly conceived, in France and the English-speaking world. It brings together scholars from different disciplines — philosophers, literary critics, political theorists — younger thinkers

Paragraph 34.3 (2011): 287–300
DOI: 10.3366/para.2011.0026
© Edinburgh University Press
www.eupjournals.com/para

and established specialists of his philosophy. While the collection
is not intended as a defence or an expression of allegiance to
Wittgenstein's work (it is marked by scepticism about *maîtres à penser*
in whatever form), it does hope to help conceptualize and historicize
the philosophical and ideological allegiances in what has long been
known in Anglophone academia as 'Theory', and suggest alternative
trajectories of critical thinking from the immediate post-war period to
the present.

In the English-speaking world, Wittgenstein has been, for the most
part, vital to theorizing in the humanities and social sciences since the
1960s. The Wittgenstinian idea of a 'form of life' has been particularly
fecund in anthropological writings since the publication, in 1973, of
Clifford Geertz's *The Interpretation of Cultures*. Geertz presses the key
Wittgenstinian concepts of the 'language game' and 'form of life'
into service in elaborating his theory of the 'thick description' of
cultural phenomena.[3] To take a second example, Quentin Skinner has
made Wittgenstein's philosophy — joined with J.L. Austin's speech-act
theory — a point of departure for historical analysis, in particular in the
domain of intellectual history, of what past writers were *doing* by means
of their utterances. These theoretical uses of Wittgenstein's thought
have had a wide resonance, although they have been controversial.[4] My
own way into Wittgenstein has been through concerns about historical
interpretation and hermeneutics, in particular the questions of how we
might know — and whether we can know — what 'forms of life' are
reflected in texts written in the distant past.

While Wittgenstein's influence within history and anthropology
has been decisive, in literary studies and philosophy his position has
been contested. On the one hand, there has been important writing
on literature inspired by Wittgenstinian models: an early example is
Stanley Cavell's 1969 *Must We Mean What We Say*;[5] more recently,
literary critics such as Charles Altieri[6] and Marjorie Perloff[7] have taken
Wittgenstein as a fruitful point of departure.[8] But the Wittgenstinian
tradition has not been central to recent literary critical practice. Part of
the story is no doubt the way the ambivalent 1960s French reception
of Wittgenstein has shaped how his writings have been read (or not
read) within English-language 'Theory', based largely on those same
French philosophers. 'Theory', as such, has also been moulded by the
antagonisms within the English-speaking academies, not only within
philosophy (across, for example, the analytical/continental divide), but
also between disciplines (literary studies and philosophy). In Anglo-
American philosophy departments themselves, although in quite a
different vein, there has been much interest in (but also considerable

scepticism about) the enduring value of Wittgenstein's philosophy, which nonetheless has played a central role in the history of the discipline, above all in the three decades following the publication, in 1953, of the *Philosophical Investigations*.

Despite, or because, of these tensions, Wittgenstein's work casts a revealing light on the activities of interpretation and understanding and provides a instructive reference point for analysis. I return to the French case as a significant one, precisely because Wittgenstein has had a later, and troubled, reception in that country. Temporally speaking, the influence of the philosopher stands in something like an inverse mirror image of Wittgenstein reception in the English-speaking world. Wittgenstein's thought was largely, although not entirely, unknown in France at the moment when its influence in English-language philosophy was at its height. Wittgenstein was certainly not central to the work of the grand theoreticians of the late 1960s, dominated instead — as Vincent Descombes put it more than thirty years ago — first by their relationship to the 'three H's' (Hegel, Husserl and Heidegger) and then to the 'three masters of suspicion' (Marx, Nietzsche and Freud).[9] He was not entirely unknown, however, and a number of articles in this collection touch on his French reception, showing a counter-current of engagement with his philosophy. The *Tractatus Logico-Philosophicus* (1921/1922) was translated with the *Philosophical Investigations* (1953), by Pierre Klossowski (imperfectly); the volume appeared in 1961. Michel de Certeau, Jean-François Lyotard, Pierre Bourdieu, Jacques Lacan and Vincent Descombes have all engaged, to various extents, with Wittgenstein's philosophy. Jacques Bouveresse's 1976 *Le Mythe de l'intériorité* is the first large-scale French work on Wittgenstein. Bouveresse's philosophy, of which, unfortunately, little has been translated into English, is anything but marginal in France: the philosopher has held a chair at the Collège de France, France's most prestigious academic body, since 1995 (he became an emeritus professor in 2010). In recent times, Wittgenstein has become central to French philosophical reflection; in particular, he has inspired much French thinking of an ethical and aesthetic cast. The work of Sandra Laugier and Christine Chauviré has been influenced by Wittgensteinians such as Stanley Cavell and Cora Diamond and has often emphasized ethical issues such as self-transformation.[10] The Wittgensteinian trajectory in France is more extended than one might originally have thought.

Alain Badiou's collection, *L'Antiphilosophie de Wittgenstein*, a preface and two essays of unequal length, which appeared in an English translation in 2011, is perhaps the French reading of Wittgenstein that will attract the most attention in English-language critical theory in the near future.[11] The texts have their origin in a quartet of lecture courses given at the Ecole Normale Supérieure (rue d'Ulm) in Paris in the 1990s (on Nietzsche, Wittgenstein, Lacan and St Paul). As one would be amiss not to include such an important discussant of Wittgenstein in this collection, it is worth looking in some detail at these essays. But first some more general words about Wittgenstein.

Although it is contested, a distinction is often drawn between Wittgenstein's 'early' and 'late' periods. Briefly stated, the 'early' Wittgenstein is generally seen as presenting a totalizing picture of language and its relationship — one of representation — to the world of 'facts'; the second Wittgenstein is seen as containing a particularized investigation of linguistic phenomena no longer viewed as a unity or according to the assumption of representation. Two works are seen as emblematic of these periods; the first is the *Tractatus Logico-Philosophicus* — published in 1921 in the last issue of Wilhelm Ostwald's *Annalen der Naturphilosophie* and then again in a revised version — Wittgenstein had not overseen the first printing — in 1922, with a preface by Bertrand Russell. The second is the posthumous *Philosophical Investigations*, assembled by Wittgenstein's students G.E.M. Anscombe and Rush Rhees and published in 1953, two years after the philosopher's death.[12] The period between these two major texts brought forth a large amount of writing often thought to be preliminary studies for the *Investigations*, in particular the *Blue* and *Brown Books* and the series of fragments initially published in 1964 as *Philosophische Bemerkungen* (and later in English under the title *Philosophical Remarks*). There is a substantial *Nachlass* of collected notes.

Wittgenstein had a decidedly untraditional academic career. Born in 1889, the youngest son of a prominent, cultivated, wealthy, converted Jewish family in Vienna, he studied engineering in Berlin (1906) and Manchester (1908–10) before his interest in logic and the philosophy of mathematics brought him to Bertrand Russell in Cambridge in 1911. Russell, who seems not immediately to have warmed to Wittgenstein (and was later to fall out with his former student), was quickly impressed: Wittgenstein became a friend and collaborator. But Wittgenstein, with the outbreak of the First World War, was obliged to leave England for Austria. During the war years he served as a foot soldier and sketched out the ideas that were to become the *Tractatus Logico-Philosophicus*. Believing that the *Tractatus* had definitively solved all philosophical problems,[13] he gave up philosophy (he seems in any case to have viewed university life with suspicion and distaste). In the early 1920s, he became (rather unsuccessfully) a schoolteacher for a time in rural Austria; later he tried his hand as well at architecture (he designed a house for his sister Margarethe, completed in 1928, which still stands at Kundmanngasse 19 in Vienna). Although in the 1920s Wittgenstein had some contact with philosophical interlocutors, notably the young British logician and mathematician Frank Ramsey and the group of logical positivist philosophers eventually known as the Vienna Circle (in particular Moritz Schlick), it is only in 1929 that he returned to Cambridge and to philosophy, offering the *Tractatus*, which he already saw as seriously flawed, as a PhD thesis. (G.E. Moore wrote in his examiner's report: 'It is my personal opinion that Mr Wittgenstein's thesis is a work of genius, but, be that as it may, it is certainly well up to the standard required for the Cambridge degree of Doctor of Philosophy.')[14] Wittgenstein received a five-year fellowship from Trinity College, Cambridge, which expired in June 1936. The three years after his Trinity fellowship expired were peripatetic, spent between Norway, Vienna and Cambridge. However, in early 1939, Wittgenstein was appointed Professor of Philosophy at Cambridge, succeeding G.E. Moore, a position he would hold until the end of 1947, although he spent some of the war in voluntary hospital work in London. Wittgenstein, whose health was failing, resigned his professorship to dedicate himself to his writing. He travelled quite a bit in his final years, staying at some length in Ireland, Norway, Austria and the US, in addition to some time in Cambridge, where he died of cancer in April 1951.[15]

The unorthodox character of Wittgenstein's relationship to university institutions appeals to Alain Badiou, who quite explicitly sets himself up in opposition to what he terms 'academic' philosophy. Badiou's first essay, with the same title as the collection, 'L'Antiphilosophie de Wittgenstein', is the longer of the two, putting forward Badiou's positions on the *Tractatus*, a work he admires, though he believes it emblematic of Wittgenstein's 'antiphilosophy'. The second, much shorter, entitled 'Les langues de Wittgenstein', is concerned both with the *Tractatus* and the *Philosophical Investigations*. Badiou's reading of the later Wittgenstein is generally hostile. Badiou explains, in the preface:

I envisioned composing a triptych: the text on Wittgenstein's styles would have functioned as a caesura and a meditation between the analyses of the two most important 'books' (the second never having become a book, at least not during Wittgenstein's life-time) of this tormented antiphilosopher: the *Tractatus* on the one hand, and the *Philosophical Investigations* on the other. Some desperate, discouraging attempts, taken up again from an ever-greater distance, have not produced anything of interest concerning the *Investigations*. To tell the truth, as my readers moreover will be able to see for themselves, I do not really like this later book, and even less so, I must say, what it has become, to wit: the involuntary, undeserved guarantee of Anglo-American grammarian philosophy — that twentieth-century form of scholasticism, as impressive for its institutional force as it is contrary to everything that Wittgenstein the mystic, the aesthete, the Stalinist of spirituality, could have desired. (*WA*, 70–1)[16]

Badiou consistently distinguishes between 'philosophy', 'antiphilosophy' and 'sophism' in his analysis of Wittgenstein. Whereas 'antiphilosophy' is a useful spur to philosophical reflection, ultimately to be overcome by philosophy, 'sophism', although it can co-exist with antiphilosophy, is not reconcilable to philosophy's commitment to truth. Although Badiou sees the first Wittgenstein as a valuable antiphilosopher — and provides a penetrating close reading of the *Tractatus* — he reads the later Wittgenstein as imbued by sophism, denying that the later work has useful philosophical content.[17] Badiou's dislike for the *Investigations*, and the Anglo-American, 'grammarian' and 'scholastic' philosophy he detests, is set up against a series of epithets combining mysticism and Stalinism (used apparently as a positive term, no doubt purposefully in order to raise eyebrows). Although Badiou dislikes the *Philosophical Investigations*, it does not prevent him from echoing Wittgenstein's rhetorical strategy in his own preface, when he admits that he has been unable to carry through his original project. Wittgenstein had written: 'after several unsuccessful attempts to weld my results together into (. . .) a whole, I realized that I should never succeed' (*PI*, Preface, 3ᵉ).

In his second essay, Badiou gives his reasons for rejecting — quite violently — the style and substance of the later Wittgenstein:

The languages themselves — without entering into too much detail — are also different. Wittgenstein's first language is at bottom that of Nietzsche, a language of the great noon of affirmation, whose signifying unity is the aphorism and whose paradigm is the quivering impassivity of the poem. It is a form of German that is both tortured and imperial. The second, highly marked by the didactic element and the perpetual inquiry, of which English is the underlying model, is a deliberately minor language, which holds any affirmation that is overly solidified into the phrase to be a metaphysical impoliteness. (*WA*, 172)[18]

Badiou elaborates this distinction (between the language of the *Tractatus*, founded on a commanding affirmation akin to poetic expression, and that of the *Philosophical Investigations*, constantly interrogative, which eschews assertion as inherently unseemly), by questioning the character of Wittgenstein's later writing as a variety of 'hassling' or 'harassment':

Discursive solidity is the said presentation of the sayable. The Wittgenstein of the *Tractatus* sees its clarity in the adjustment of an ontology of objects and a logic of elementary propositions. The resulting language is an aphoristic logicism. But can we then truly signify the unsayable? Or do we obtain merely the closed montage of onto-logy? This question leads Wittgenstein to replace the onto-logical disposition with an experimental anthropological pluralism, to replace the rhetoric of affirmation with that of the approximative hassling. But do we then not completely lose sight of the question of the One? Do we still know where to situate the place of empty words, God, the mystical, the divine — words whose referent, inasmuch as it is on the order of the act, is the only available value? (*WA*, 177)[19]

Indeed, Badiou is insistent about what he calls the 'massive' quality of true philosophy:

The philosophical discourse — whether we are dealing with Aristotle, Descartes or Heidegger makes no difference whatsoever in this regard — is assembled with an eye on obtaining assent, which must be extorted even by anticipating, as much as possible, the eventual objections. Whence a syntax that is always solid, in the sense of endlessly hitting the same nail or, to be more precise, of ensuring that, no matter how one holds the hammer, it is always the same nail that gets knocked in. In this regard, the more a philosophy declares itself 'open', deconstructive, or even sceptical, the more rigorous are the artifices of its brooding. There is nothing syntactically more monotonous than the exhortations to liberate oneself from destiny or to undo metaphysics. Philosophy (no matter its otherwise trumpeted declarations about the freedom of mind) organizes its discourse in such a way as to leave no opening through which heterogeneity might pass, nor any clearing through which deception could filter itself. (*WA*, 165)[20]

The valorization of the 'massive' quality of poetry and philosophical discourse — one which suggests, to Badiou, the striking formulation that the *Tractatus* is like Rimbaud's ' "A Season in Hell" rewritten in the language of Mallarmé's "A Throw of the Dice" ' (*WA*, 169) — transforms into sophism any philosophical discourse that does not assert, but rather questions. In later Wittgenstein, Badiou argues that such language is purely evasive: 'The second style, the bee style — torment and relaunch — follows diagonal lines of flight without logic or proof, suspending the rhetoric from the evasive form of the question and the question of the question' (*WA*, 178).[21]

We see in Badiou's interpretation of Wittgenstein the defence of a variety of philosophy that distrusts questioning and strongly valorizes affirmation. The *Tractatus*'s assertion is far superior to the *Investigations*'s questioning, since, as Badiou insists:

The philosopher assumes the voice of the master. Philosophers are not, nor can they be, modest participants in team work, laborious instructors of a closed history, democrats given over to public debates. Their word is authoritarian, as seductive as it is violent, committing others to follow suit, disturbing and converting them. Philosophers are present, as such, in what they state; even if this presence is also that of an exemplary submission, they do not subtract themselves from the duty of reason. (*WA*, 68)[22]

Perhaps such a definition of philosophy will not appeal to all readers. In any case, Badiou's assertion demands a longer comment, since it can be read in at least two ways. Firstly, in a way that recuperates Badiou's argument but removes its teeth, in terms of the methods by which a philosophical voice will ideally foreclose, through the strength of its argumentation, anticipated responses, being (this is Wittgenstein's own attitude regarding the *Tractatus*) the victorious word in an agon of philosophical discussion rendering future conversation both unnecessary and impertinent. This would be the idea of the philosopher as the resolver of intractable problems, the clearer of thorny fields, the dissolver of nebulous confusions. Secondly — and this is no doubt closer to the violence of Badiou's claim — the philosopher bears the name of an emerging imperative truth — *aux grands hommes la philosophie reconnaissante* ! — imposing itself as an authority demanding only the awed silence of a terrified animal. Truth in mathematics, poetry, as in philosophy and politics, monolithic in character—a calm bloc of dark stone fallen to earth — has the indubitable character of massive materiality. There certainly is a striking contrast between Bruno Bosteels's careful discussion of Badiou's text, which occupies the first third of the English translation, and the choices of the book-designers offering 'Praise for Alain Badiou' extracted from prominent current thinkers. Such adulation of the philosopher's name fits remarkably well with the market logic of publishing fashion and the university, however strongly Badiou's philosophy itself might oppose such forces.

Badiou's valorization of the *Tractatus*, and its totalizing theoretical ambitions, reflects a very long tradition in French reception of

Wittgenstein, in which the *Investigations* were not always easily assimilated and the *Tractatus*, even when unread and/or taken as an object of scorn, has been much better known.[23] But beyond Badiou's rejection of the form of Wittgenstein's later work is a commitment to a particular view of the philosophical voice, one that he sees as instantiated in the work of the first Wittgenstein and dissipated in the second. Certainly, the privileging of the mathematical and logical model within the work of the first Wittgenstein — however misguided Badiou thinks Wittgenstein's views of mathematics and logic — informs Badiou's rejection of the dominant sophism of the *Investigations* in favour of the massive (anti)- philosophy of the *Tractatus*.

The view of Wittgenstein in the present volume is not monolithic. This collection does not offer Wittgenstein as an exemplary theoretical discourse through which texts and other cultural objects *should* be read. The idea is not to be Wittgenstinian in the sense of following the call of a philosophical voice (or indeed in protecting him from attacks, such as those of Deleuze or Badiou, on his philosophy). Rather, the point is to show how Wittgenstein remains, for a number of critics from several different traditions, a crucial point of reference for questions of ethics, aesthetics and interpretation.

The essays presented fall into two groups. The first address the relationship of Wittgenstein to French philosophy and the history of what is broadly called 'Theory' in the English-speaking world; the second consider the relationship of Wittgenstein's philosophy to literary and musical interpretation.

Jacques Bouveresse, long the most prominent French commentator on Wittgenstein, has contributed an extended article on the suspicious views of questions of progress articulated by the Viennese satirist Karl Kraus, his avid reader Ludwig Wittgenstein and the latter's student (and successor as professor of philosophy at Cambridge) Georg Henrik von Wright.

Sandra Laugier has written a tribute to one of Wittgenstein's most important French readers, the distinguished specialist of ancient philosophy Pierre Hadot. Laugier shows how Hadot, who published some of the earliest work on Wittgenstein's later philosophy to appear in French, found in Wittgenstein a profoundly fruitful approach to ethical philosophy. Hadot's theorizing of spiritual exercises — which resembles in many important respects later reflections on Wittgenstein's philosophy such as those of Stanley Cavell and Cora Diamond (and was an important influence on Michel Foucault's late work on the 'care of the self') — conceives of philosophy as a living praxis.

James Helgeson examines the early reception of Wittgenstein in France, contextualizing the relatively rare early reactions by contrast to the long-standing centrality of Wittgenstinian themes in much English-speaking philosophy. Taking into account a variety of early work in French on Wittgenstein, the article reflects upon the influence in France of Wittgenstinian ideas in the period before 1967.

Reidar Due contributes a discussion of the philosophical differences between Gilles Deleuze and Ludwig Wittgenstein, two thinkers whom he considers intellectually incompatible. Due enumerates some of the differences between the two thinkers and argues that Deleuze would have been profoundly hostile to a variety of 'pragmatism' he finds latent in Wittgenstein and openly expressed in his followers.

Jonathan Havercroft contributes a spirited defence of Quentin Skinner's methodological practice. Skinner, following a cue from Wittgenstein, suggests that in interpreting texts of the past what we do is attempt to understand what the authors of those texts were *doing* by writing them. Havercoft argues that a noted recent article by Peter Steinberger misjudges both Skinner's critical *enjeux* and his methodological reference points. Havercroft's article, in particular, distances the question of speech–act theory from Derridean formulations of speech and writing, which many philosophers (including, for example, Badiou, who addresses the question directly in the essay on Wittgenstein's style)[24] have not always found pertinent.

Garry Hagberg, a distinguished specialist on Wittgenstinian aesthetics, contributes an article on music and meaning in a Wittgenstinian perspective. His article rests on a comparison between the ideas expressed in the self-enclosed world of the *Tractatus* and the musical theories of the influential Heinrich Schenker, a Viennese theorist of tonality, and those of his contemporary Arnold Schoenberg. (Wittgenstein, whose taste in music was conservative, had no sympathy for Schoenberg's aesthetic innovations.)

Alison James takes Wittgenstein's later philosophy as a point of departure for the examination of French surrealism and the philosophy of the everyday. In studying the poetics of André Breton and Louis Aragon in a Wittgenstinian framework, in the spirit of what Stanley Cavell has called the 'surrealism of the habitual', James suggests that the philosophy illuminates the surrealist project in its conflicted relationship to 'ordinary language', valued, as in Wittgenstein, as a possible refuge against the temptations of scepticism.

Finally, Maria Muresan gives a detailed account of how two of the most significant recent French poets, Henri Meschonnic and Jacques Roubaud, have engaged with Wittgenstein's philosophy as an alternative to the dominant post-structuralist discourses of their generation. Meschonnic's reading of Wittgenstein is, for Muresan, a sustained, rigorous, but a highly critical one. Roubaud's reading of Wittgenstein, by contrast, is linked to the poet's grief following the death, in 1983, of his wife, Alix, a photographer very deeply invested in Wittgenstinian philosophy.[25]

Wittgenstein is a key figure for explaining the problematic relationship between what is still often called 'analytic' philosophy in Anglo-American circles and the tradition of 'Theory' often inspired by so-called 'continental' thinkers. This is a debate that remains current, in particular in the unfortunate contemporary circumstances for university funding, where broad solidarity across the humanities should now be *de mise*. Much recent work on Wittgenstein, both in English and French, is ethical in cast. '*Du mußt dein leben ändern*' ('You must change your life'), Rilke tells us.[26] Wittgenstein says the same, in more or less the same words: 'all good doctrines are useless: you must change your life' (cited in *LW*, 490). Yet the philosophy cannot only be transformed into a peculiar kind of latter-day neo-Stoicism or, much worse, self-help — or, in Badiou's critical formulation 'an interior event within its own thought' (*WA*, 180)[27] — that negates political responsibility and action. It is this apolitical Wittgenstein that Badiou wishes (and, in another vein, both Jacques Bouveresse and Sandra Laugier strongly desire) to counter, and what Badiou calls Wittgenstein's latent despair. In his concluding chapter to his essay on the *Tractatus*, Badiou touches on the question of what he calls 'salvation', common, he asserts, to Heidegger and Wittgenstein. Such 'salvation' could all too easily be identified as an inner affair of comfortable self-contemplation, negating intersubjective, public resistance. Against this, the strong political orientation of Badiou's reading of Wittgenstein is exemplary.

NOTES

1 Transcribed from the video interview with Claire Parnet directed by Pierre-André Boutang: 'Je ne veux pas parler de ça. Pour moi c'est une catastrophe philosophique (...) c'est (...) une régression massive de toute la philosophie. C'est très triste, l'affaire Wittgenstein. (...) Ils ont foutu un système de terreur où sous prétexte de faire quelque chose de nouveau (...) c'est la pauvreté

instaurée en grandeur. Il n'y a pas de mot pour décrire ce danger-là. (...).
C'est grave, surtout qu'ils sont méchants les wittgensteiniens, et puis ils cassent
tout. S'ils l'emportent, alors là il y aura un assassinat de la philosophie — s'ils
l'emportent. C'est des assassins de la philosophie. Il faut une grande vigilance.'
My translation. DVD: Gilles Deleuze and Claire Parnet, *L'Abécédaire de Gilles
Deleuze* (Paris: Editions Montparnasse-Regards, 2004).

2   There is indeed in France a very marked upswing in interest in Wittgenstein
as well as post-Wittgenstinian language philosophy in the 'analytic' tradition,
as recent translations of Wittgenstein as well as classic texts within the
'analytic' tradition (e.g. Quine, Davidson) attest (and, in a very different vein,
Alain Badiou's lectures on Wittgenstein as an 'anti-philosopher', published in
French in 2009, of which more later in this introduction).

3   Clifford Geertz, *The Interpretation of Cultures* (New York: Basic Books, 1973),
in particular ch. 1.

4   See Quentin Skinner, *Visions of Politics: Vol. 1. Regarding Method* (Cambridge:
Cambridge University Press, 2002).

5   Stanley Cavell, *Must We Mean What We Say* (Cambridge: Cambridge
University Press, 1969, revised edition 2002).

6   Charles Altieri, 'Wittgenstein on Consciousness and Language: A Challenge
to Derridean Theory', *MLN*, 91 (1976), 1397–1423. Reprinted in
Wittgenstein, Theory, and the Arts, edited by Richard Allen and Malcolm
Turvey (London: Routledge, 2001), 230–53.

7   Marjorie Perloff, *Wittgenstein's Ladder: Poetic Language and the Strangeness of the
Ordinary* (Chicago: University of Chicago Press, 1996).

8   I have avoided here the term 'ordinary language philosophy' which is too
narrowly focussed on a tradition — what Emile Benveniste, in 1963, called
'la philosophie d'Oxford' — associated with the 1950s and in particular with
J.L. Austin. It is not that Wittgenstein was not a significant influence on
this current of philosophy, or that Austin's philosophy (like that of Grice)
is not, in some sense, an offshoot of the Wittgenstinian tradition broadly
understood. But Wittgenstein is not just an 'ordinary language philosopher'.
See, however, the useful website on 'Ordinary Langauge and Literary Studies'
at http://olponline.wordpress.com/, consulted 12 July 2011, 3:05 a.m.

9   Vincent Descombes, *Modern French Philosophy* (Cambridge: Cambridge
University Press, 1980), 3 (original edition *Le Même et l'autre* (Paris:
Minuit, 1979)). Wittgenstein's name does not appear at all in Descombes's
study, although he has since been a distinguished French commentator on
Wittgenstein, and, to be sure, Wittgenstein is not completely absent from
French thought prior to 1980.

10   Much of the work in this volume will engage, in particular, with Cavell's
philosophy.

11   The text appeared first in a German version by Heiko Jatho in 2008, in
French in 2009 and in an English translation by Bruno Bosteels in the

summer of 2011. Alain Badiou, *Wittgensteins Antiphilosophie* (Zürich/Berlin: diaphanes, 2008), *L'Antiphilosophie de Wittgenstein* (Caen: Nous, 2009), *Wittenstein's Antiphilosophy* (New York: Verso, 2011), henceforward *WA*. I quote from Bosteels's recent translation and give the original French page numbers in footnotes.

12 The translation of the *Investigations*, for almost sixty years the standard English text, has recently been considerably revised by P.M.S. Hacker and Joachim Schulte (the latter has also published a critical edition of the German text of the *Investigations*). Ludwig Wittgenstein, *Philosophical Investigations*. The German text with an English translation by G.E.M. Anscombe, P.M.S. Hacker and Joachim Schulte (Oxford: Wiley/Blackwell, 2009); *Philosophische Untersuchungen: Kritisch-genetische Edition*, edited by Joachim Schulte (Frankfurt am Main: Suhrkamp, 2001). The *Philosophical Investigations* will be referred to henceforward as *PI*, followed by the paragraph number. The Hacker/Schulte edition is very new, and there is not yet consensus about which edition is the standard one. Authors in this volume have made their own choices regarding editons. These choices are noted in the endnotes.

13 'The truth of the thoughts communicated here seems to me unassailable and definitive. I am, therefore, of the opinion that the problems have in essentials been finally solved. And if I am not mistaken in this, then the value of this work secondly consists in the fact that it shows how little has been done when these problems have been solved.' *Tractatus Logico-Philosophicus*, preface, translated by Cecil K. Ogden. The text is here taken from Jonathan Witt's hypertext edition of the *Tractatus* at http://www.kfs.org/~jonathan/witt/tlph.html, consulted 11 July 2011, 4:35 p.m. The *Tractatus*, in this volume, will henceforward be referred to as *TLP* followed by the number of the proposition.

14 Ray Monk, *Ludwig Wittgenstein: The Duty of Genius* (London: Penguin, 1991), 272, henceforward *LW*.

15 The standard biographies of Wittgenstein are those of Ray Monk and (for the early period) Brian McGuinness, *Young Ludwig: Wittgenstein's Life, 1889–1921* (Oxford: Oxford University Press, 2005). Cambridge University maintains a timeline of the philosopher's life. Start page: http://www.wittgen-cam.ac.uk/biogre1.html, consulted 12 July 2011, 2:35 a.m.

16 Badiou, *L'Antiphilosophie de Wittgenstein*, 10.

17 Badiou's rejection of the later Wittgenstein is not unique to him; indeed Bertrand Russell had caustically claimed that 'the later Wittgenstein seems to have grown tired of serious thinking and to have invented a doctrine which would make such an activity unnecessary. I do not for one moment believe that the doctrine which has these lazy consequences is true. The desire to

understand the world is, they think, an outdated folly.' Bertrand Russell, *My Philosophical Development* (London: Unwin Books, 1959), 161.

18   Badiou, *L'Antiphilosophie de Wittgenstein*, 105.

19   Badiou, *L'Antiphilosophie de Wittgenstein*, 110.

20   Badiou, *L'Antiphilosophie de Wittgenstein*, 98

21   Badiou, *L'Antiphilosophie de Wittgenstein*, 111.

22   Badiou, *L'Antiphilosophie de Wittgenstein*, 8.

23   In Pierre Klossowski's translation of the two major philosophical works of Wittgenstein, the *Tractatus* gets very clear top billing. This edition, however faulty, does have the advantage of grouping together, as Wittgenstein himself suggested, the first work with the second. This has not been the case in recent editions of Wittgenstein, either the revised text of P.M.S. Hacker or the recent edition of what are called the *Recherches philosophiques*, prepared by a team of translators under the supervision of E. Rigal (Paris: Gallimard, 2004).

24   Badiou, *L'Antiphilosophie de Wittgenstein*, 97.

25   The pieces by James and Muresan arise from a panel on Wittgenstein and literature that we organized for the Modern Language Association Convention in Philadelphia in December 2009.

26   Rainer Maria Rilke, 'Archaïscher Torso Apollos', l. 14. In *Gedichte* (Leipzig: Insel Verlag, 1955), 557.

27   Badiou, *L'Antiphilosophie de Wittgenstein*, 113.

Wittgenstein, von Wright and the Myth of Progress[1]

Jacques Bouveresse

Abstract:

The Viennese satirist Karl Kraus called progress a 'standpoint that looks like movement' and a 'mobile decoration': a politically useful slogan devoid of content. Despite his tendency to think in the revolutionary mode of the *tabula rasa*, Ludwig Wittgenstein was a cultural conservative, sceptical of progress. He shares this pessimistic scepticism with some, but not all, of the early twentieth-century Viennese writers he read enthusiastically (strong sceptics include Kraus but not Robert Musil). It would, however, be too simple to claim that Wittgenstein did not believe in the possibility of progress. Rather, he thought it mistaken to confuse progress with continued movement in one direction. Georg Henrik von Wright, Wittgenstein's student and successor at Cambridge, has discussed the 'myth of progress' in Wittgenstinian terms; the relevance of these analyses of progress in contemporary political discourse is examined.

Keywords: progress, Wittgenstein, Karl Kraus, Robert Musil, Georg Henrik von Wright, Vienna

'Under the sign of Progress'

In 1909, Karl Kraus published, initially in *Simplicissimus* and then in number 275–76 of *Die Fackel*,[2] a famous article entitled 'Der Fortschritt' ('Progress') that Wittgenstein may have read. The gist of the argument may be summed up thus: for its author, progress is at most a mere form, and probably even much less than that, in other words a cliché or a slogan, but certainly devoid of content. Kraus begins by explaining with irony that—thanks to the newspapers—he has finally understood what progress is. Progress isn't movement,

Paragraph 34.3 (2011): 301–321
DOI: 10.3366/para.2011.0027
© Edinburgh University Press
www.eupjournals.com/para

but rather a state, consisting in 'feeling ahead' no matter what one does, yet without the need to advance. In the term 'Fortschritt,' the prefix 'fort-' signifies being in front and the word 'Schritt' that steps are taken, but there is nothing in what we call progress that allows us to perceive it as stepping forward:

A newspaper phrase conveying a lively image has suggested itself to me. This is how it is worded: we are under the sign of progress. Only now do I recognize progress for what it is — a mobile decoration. We stay ahead and keep walking in place. Progress is a standpoint (*Standpunkt*) and looks like movement. Only occasionally does something twist itself around in front of my eyes: it is a dragon guarding a hoard of gold. Or else it moves around through the streets at night: that's the street sweeper's rolling broom that stirs up the dust of the day, so that it will settle somewhere else. Wherever I went, I couldn't help but run into it. If I went back, it came at me from the other side, and I recognized that a political program contrary to progress was useless, because progress is the unavoidable development of dust. Fate floats in a cloud, and progress, which catches up to you when you think you're getting away from it, comes from over there like the *Deus ex machina*. It slips through and reaches the fleeing foot and in the process takes as much dust out of your way as it is necessary to spread so that all lungs have their share in it, for the machine serves the great progressive idea of spreading dust. In the end, though, the full meaning of progress occurred to me while it was raining. It was raining unceasingly and humanity was thirsty for dust. There was none, and the street sweeper couldn't stir it up. But behind it, a water cart followed deliberately, not letting the rain deter it from preventing the dust that couldn't develop. That was progress.[3]

Kraus describes progress as the prototype for a mechanical or quasi-mechanical process, self-sustaining and self-maintained, that creates in each instance the conditions of its own perpetuation, in particular by producing drawbacks, inconveniences and damages that only new progress can enable us to overcome. The fact that, as von Wright states, 'continuous economic growth is a condition of the solution to the problems that intensified and rationalized industrial production itself creates,'[4] is a typical illustration. It would seem that additional growth is necessary to solve the problems posed by growth, particularly in matters of the damage inflicted to the environment and of the worsening poverty that reigns in certain regions of the world. For example, those who currently manifest reluctance regarding the use of GMOs can consequently be charged with being enemies of science and progress, but may also be suspected of wanting, in a way, to starve the population of the third world. This is the kind of circle in which most current debates on such questions turn. Adversaries of the dogma of unlimited growth are thereby compelled to a certain degree of caution; but this circle also considerably weakens the position of the advocates of the dogma, because their foremost advantage is that the real and considerable improvements that might follow on a thoughtful and judicious use of what is gained through growth can always be held over to the next day and even deferred indefinitely. Partisans of ultra-liberalism in matters of economics maintain that wealthy countries must become even wealthier so that poor countries might (perhaps) have a chance to become a bit less poor. But, in addition to the fact that one can, in spite of it all, consider oneself entitled to demand a bit more in matters of equality and justice, one must have real faith to believe in what they promise us. Kraus suggests that a fraction of the intellectual energy that the contemporary world devotes to what we call 'progress' should rather be used to consider what should be done with the advantages it procures us, and to direct their use to more serious and pressing purposes. But, as he says, when the question asked is no longer that of progress, but rather that of determining what to do with it, faith suffices and proof can wait. And it is a faith that unconditional advocates of progress — or perhaps, to be exact, of growth — seem to be able to count on now more than ever.

A sceptical mind, on the other hand, might be tempted to conclude, in Kraus's fashion, that the real goal of progress, if there is one, has finally become clear: all things proceed as if this goal were actually none other than the continuation of progress itself. But what exactly is this thing we call progress? Kraus's observation is that progress, under the sign of which we are supposed to be marching, was perhaps for a time something real, but is today nothing more than an obligatory representation corresponding to a content we can no longer grasp:

How does it reveal itself to the light of day? In what shape does it show itself when we think of it as an agile servant of the times? For we have obligated ourselves to such a representation, we would like to become aware of progress, and all we are missing is the perception of the thing that we are convinced of. Of all the things that walk and run and ride, we see only feet, hooves, wheels. The tracks efface themselves. Here a stock exchange errand runner rushed by, over there an apocalyptic rider hunted. In vain... We can speak on the telephone from Schmuck-wit to Toadying,[5] but we don't yet know what progress looks like. All we know is that it didn't influence the quality of long distance communication. And once we have come to the point of believing that thoughts can be transferred between Vienna and Berlin, if we are unable to be in awe of this device in its perfection, it will only be because of the thoughts. Humanity is working right on target; it spends its intellectual capital on its inventions and saves nothing for their operation. But simply because of this, progress is already one of the most meaningful inventions that humanity has succeeded in creating, because to make it work only belief is necessary, and so those advocates of progress who lay claim to unlimited credit have the winning hand. ('Der Fortschritt', 198)

In other words, where progress is concerned, we never perceive anything more than movement in all directions and at ever-increasing speed, but no movement that corresponds to the idea we have of progress. Victor Hugo wrote that, 'the collective stride of the human race is called Progress. Progress advances.'[6] In any case, that is indeed what the word suggests, in English, French and German alike. But, for Kraus, among all the things that walk or rather run today, progress is indeed the one thing that cannot be said to be in running order. It is not the aim we aspire to that justifies speed and acceleration in all the things, which currently constitute the symbols *par excellence* of progress, rather such things have now become the goal. 'It was', Kraus says, 'as if it were not an aim that ordered the hurry of the world, but rather hurry signified the aim of the world' ('Der Fortschritt', 202). As all critics of progress have in different ways, and as von Wright does today, Kraus emphasizes that it seems that the means have definitively taken precedence over the ends: as the means became more and more inordinate, the ends have become more and more indefinite and impossible to perceive. But if progress resides now only in the means, which do indeed have a tendency to grow constantly, it is not surprising that we should come across it at every step, with the sense that each time we really encounter something else. The impression resulting from what happens is that progress is everywhere, while its physiognomy can nevertheless no longer be recognized anywhere. As Kraus puts it, there is no way to escape it, since in our current societies everything is done in a new way, and even anything done at all is placed under the sign of progress, while the faces it presents to us are no longer anything more than disguises which render it unrecognizable. It is as if we were walking around in a place that rented masks. There seems to be a face hidden behind them, but it has been a long time since we knew anything about what it might resemble.

Using here, as he often does, the satirical device of boiling things down to the concrete, Kraus deliberately avoids bringing up the issue of the general idea of progress. According to him, we obviously can't get anything out of it, and he effectively concerns himself only with figures, which for an ingenuous questioner seem to give a tangible image of progress. But when one proceeds in this way, one is suddenly in strange and ill-assorted company. In the house of progress, everything is under the sign of ambiguity and ambivalence, and can cohabit with anything. As soon as concrete illustrations are taken into account, we realize that in progress there is always both something moving forward and something moving backward, and that even if one feels compelled to believe in progress, we never quite succeed in determining whether it is the forward or the backward that wins out. One of Kraus's numerous ironic examples of how he encounters progress is a lady laden with necklaces who explains that the cheapest way to hear the Ninth Symphony is to go to the blue-collar concert, but that to do so, one must dress like an indigent. That, says Kraus, was progress; and apparently, according to him, for someone who naively asks what progress is today, such a response is neither better nor worse than any other.

'Progress', von Wright tells us, 'is distinctly a value notion. In this it differs from related concepts such as change and growth — and also from development. These latter are (or may be treated as) purely factual. That one state of affairs represents progress in comparison with another (. . .) is, however, not anything which can be established by scientific argument or otherwise on the basis of facts about the things in question.'[7] In this context, there is of course no question of instrumental value judgements regarding the more or less appropriate character of a means to a given end, which are generally based on facts, but rather of judgements through which something is declared to be good or better in itself. If what von Wright says is correct, three important consequences directly follow: (1) The notion of progress is necessarily affected by the same kind of relativity and subjectivity as that of value in general, at least for those who contest the possibility of attributing a real and objective content to valuations. (2) Even if progress can have an objective and even factual aspect, the reality that it possesses for human beings always depends, in the last instance, on an act of evaluation whose responsibility lies with them. As Kraus would say, even if machines could not only transmit, but also, in the end, replace thought, it would still always depend on thought whether or not to consider this an improvement. One needn't be a partisan of the subjectivist conception of value to take this as an obvious truth. (3) When the reality of progress becomes a bit too imperceptible and uncertain, the idea of progress is generally replaced by one or the other of its substitutes that can be objectively grasped, and even, preferably, quantified, like, for instance, the idea of development or growth. In current discussions, this ambiguity, regularly denounced by the opponents of progress, is a constant. Someone asks, like Kraus, where one can encounter progress; and some random thing is indicated to him that, indeed, progresses, or in other words is increasing. A slightly more subtle answer consists in explaining that the opponents of unlimited growth are also opponents of progress, since the former is one of the essential preconditions of the latter. But that is a response that first presupposes the notion of progress has been endowed with a meaning that does not transform it into a simple synonym of growth.

If what the postmoderns say were true, that is that we have become thoroughly sceptical regarding the great narratives of modernity, that of progress to begin with, we would normally expect the notion of progress to be less exploited today, or in any case exploited with a bit more irony. But we need but take a look to realize that such is not at all the case. The word 'progress' has probably never been used so much, indeed it has become hackneyed, in particular in the discourse of politicians, technocrats, economists, company presidents and financiers. The obligation to serve progress has never been so pressing and the claim to do so effectively has never been so strongly asserted. Lichtenberg, whom Kraus quotes, states that he would give a lot 'to know for whose sake exactly all those things are done which are publicly said to be done for the motherland.'[8] One can, in all obviousness, ask the same question about progress. We know no doubt less and less in the name of whom or what exactly are done the multitude of things, often debatable and sometimes repellent, that are done in the name of an ideal we continue to call progress. But what is certain is that progress, as a watchword or as a slogan, has lost none of its efficacy today, even if it is often no more than a banner under which one can get an army of sanctimonious enthusiasts to march.

Musil, who unlike Kraus is a defender of scientific and technical modernity and of the heritage of the Enlightenment, notes that the current problem in the cultural area is not that our progress is nil or insufficient. Rather, while we are convinced that things progress in a quite real and satisfactory manner in our own area of specialization, we each have a tendency to consider others as not quite doing all that might be expected of them in theirs. Musil writes:

Such cultural pessimism to the detriment of others is a widespread phenomenon today. It stands in strange opposition to the power and dexterity that are deployed everywhere in the details. The impression we get from our time is quite simply that a giant, who eats, drinks and accomplishes a monstrous amount, doesn't want to have anything to do with it and listlessly proclaims he feels weak, like a young girl fatigued by her own anaemia.[9]

   This observation means that a multitude of often spectacular advances accomplished in different domains do not or no longer today add together, in the human mind, into something that would deserve the name of progress, and that the dominant impression can at the same time very well be that of stagnation or of regression. Musil states that our time creates marvels, but no longer 'feels' them. Such a situation obliges us to ask the following question: just as we are possibly formulating an erroneous value judgement when we believe ourselves to be progressing, might it not just as well be that the progress is real and that we have simply become unable to perceive and feel it? It is a question that is difficult to answer, precisely because no one has the means to determine the relationship that may exist between a sum of advances that can be characterized, and in some cases even objectively measured, and a reality, also presumed to be objective, that we would be right to call the progress of humanity or progress plain and simple. But it is clear that those who are content to, for the sake of silencing the sceptics and the pessimists, invoke the striking feats of the giant that Musil speaks of, do not answer the question of determining why they are not necessarily assessed as progress.

Are the critics of progress its enemies?

In *Science and Reason* (late 1986-early 1987), von Wright brought under scrutiny some of the most fundamental of our current beliefs, in particular the belief in progress. He reminded us, on the one hand, that the human species is subject to the same law of precariousness and extinction as other species — and nothing allows us to affirm it will not disappear in the near future, for example in a nuclear war — and on the other hand that nothing guarantees that the industrial form of production is biologically adapted to humanity, nor, more generally, that this species is still capable of adapting to an environment it has participated in transforming in such a spectacular and rapid way. These two ideas could convey the impression of being simple common sense, or in any case enlightened consciousness, and there is certainly nothing particularly shocking or subversive about them. But they have, it seems, nonetheless elicited surprising negative reactions amongst all scientists, economists, politicians, intellectuals, who share a common conviction that one might call 'the belief in unlimited economic growth'. This confirms Kraus's idea that, even if we do not know what progress is, more than ever everyone is compelled to believe that at least one thing is certain: we are progressing, we can do so indefinitely and the obligation to continue to do so is a sort of categorical imperative for contemporary societies.

When he wonders about the type of readers who would, on the contrary, be likely to appreciate the ideas he has laid out, von Wright prudently suggests two groups, designated by him as the 'value conservatives' and the 'intellectuals of the left,' about whom he observes, in a way that I certainly will not contradict, that they seem for all intents and purposes to be dying out. The question presenting itself is, in any case, to determine who the intellectuals of the left are today. Should we still call 'intellectuals of the left' people who, although generally more sensitive than others to the social and human costs of progress and in particular to the inequality, injustice and phenomena of exclusion which it engenders, nonetheless most often continue to believe in the possibility and in the necessity of progress through unlimited economic growth and are content, for the most part, to demand that the fruits of growth be distributed, if possible, a bit more equitably? On this point, the attitude of the social democrats of today and of the intellectuals that support them is not necessarily very different from that of their right-wing opponents. The case of Kraus is obviously completely different. He constitutes one of the most typical examples of membership in the group of value conservatives, which differentiates itself from that of the intellectuals of the left by rejecting the optimistic belief in the possibility of improving things, in any case of improving them by following the path of scientific and technological modernity, and by a certain tendency to consider past epochs with nostalgia. And, of course, it is also with this category that we can connect Wittgenstein.

What von Wright calls value conservatism obviously does not necessarily imply political and social conservatism, even if there is in fact a conjunction of the two most of the time, and it is also not characterized by the will to preserve, at any cost, the system of values in use. Kraus's conservatism was and remains politically ambivalent to the end and what it opposed was less a determinate system of values than a disastrous overturning that ended up placing fact above value in general. Progress can be blamed, he says, for having caused the means of living (*Lebensmittel*) to take the place of the ends of living

(*Lebenszwecke*) and life the place of the reasons for living. Progress lives to eat, but it can also very well die to eat. This is not really an exaggeration, since we are becoming more and more aware today of the fact that the excesses of consumerism, which imply and justify those of productivism, can in some cases very well become a concrete threat, not only to the survival of certain natural species, but also to that of the human species itself.

Progress, according to Kraus, tends not only to replace the essential with the incidental, but it can also perfectly well place life itself in danger in the end. In any case the idea that the only important thing is simply to consume and produce ever more can and sometimes really does lead to this type of outcome. Hence, the point is not to contest the idea that various advances can and must be made in numerous domains. Rather, in accordance with von Wright's phrase, the idea is to 'dissipate the fog surrounding the notion of progress', to challenge the conceit of the means themselves in becoming ends, while the supposed ends remain essentially indefinite and even become more and more so, and to remind us that nothing authorizes us to consider that progress should necessarily be unlimited and that there can even be vital reasons to impose limits on it right away. It is a question that, as von Wright remarks, can even be asked about the claim to knowledge, and that was asked moreover by Nietzsche, who wondered if humanity had not chosen to risk dying of knowledge and would not end up actually dying that way.

Even if, in the case of Kraus or Wittgenstein, its use corresponds without question to something real, applying the term 'conservatism' to such thinkers immediately raises a fair number of problems. Certain commentators, like J.C. Nyiri, have defended the idea that Wittgenstein's attitude displayed all the characteristics of the mode of thought we are in the habit of calling 'conservatism', and that he could be considered a representative of the neo-conservative currents that developed in the twenties, especially in Germany.[10] Indeed, at a glance there are a fair number of elements that seem to go exactly in such a direction, in particular the admiration Wittgenstein manifested for some of the most typical thinkers of the conservative tradition, like the Austrian poet Grillparzer for instance, a writer toward whom Kraus himself was much more reserved. But, as von Wright remarks, 'Wittgenstein was much more anxious to combat and distance himself from a prevailing climate of opinion than to work for the restoration of one which was already fading. He is as little nostalgic in his thinking as are Dostoevsky and Nietzsche.'[11] As von Wright himself states, Wittgenstein certainly believes neither in a brilliant future nor in the good old days.

We can, of course, if we so choose, read a certain nostalgia into some of his most typical remarks on the world and on contemporary culture, like for instance when he speaks of Schumann's time, which he states is the period corresponding to his cultural ideal.[12] But, in general, his attitude is exactly the opposite of that of the man who seeks to preserve what is or even to restore what is no longer. The assessment he articulates about the culture in which we live is that of someone who considers it condemned and who reacts to such a situation by taking Nietzsche's point of view, according to which one should never hold up, but rather push over, what is falling down. Von Wright:

The philosopher who wrote 'I destroy, I destroy, I destroy' was not alien to the thought that something new could be built once the heap of rubble of a decaying culture had been cleared away. Not unlike some radicals of the left he appears to have seen something hopeful in the drastic sweeping away of an obsolete social order that had taken place in Russia. His plans of settling in the Soviet Union can be viewed in this light too. Among his Cambridge friends in the 1930s many had a pronouncedly Marxist orientation. The only periodical which I have seen him reading and not frowning upon was 'The New Statesman and Nation' — much more in tune with the tastes of left intellectuals than with those of apolitical conservatives. (*APF* 49, 53)

Indeed, Wittgenstein seems to have had a tendency rather to think in the revolutionary mode of the *tabula rasa*, followed by a radical new beginning, than in the mode of improvement and reform that is the mode of the representatives of the idea of continual and unlimited progress. But, as von Wright remarks, it is an attitude no less opposed to that of the conservatives than it is to that of the progressivists of the usual kind. Despite his obvious and well-known pessimism, it seems to me a gross exaggeration to say that Wittgenstein did not believe in the possibility of improving things. What is true is simply that he did not believe in the possibility of improvement through continuing development in the current direction.

If we ask ourselves why the Austria Wittgenstein was born and raised in so fascinates a good portion of the intellectual world today, we can identify at least two reasons. The first is that, for people who are tired of being modern and have become sceptical regarding the very project of modernity, Kakania (*Kakanien*), as Musil calls it, offers a typical example of resistance to the project in question. As von Wright says: 'The multinational and multi-lingual state was in many ways an obsolete phenomenon in a Europe *then* on its road towards democracy and industrialization in the frames of consolidated national states. It was a reactionary bulwark against progressing modernization' (*APF* 49, 55). But the second reason why this example may seem interesting from the current point of view is precisely that 'at the same time it appears to us today strangely modern, a forecast of what may come in a Europe *now* in a process of integration with national boarders breaking down and a new mixing of languages and nationalities in the offing' (*APF* 49, 56). Since one of the chapters of von Wright's book is entitled 'It is not written in the stars that the Nation-State is the definitive form of political organization', it is not surprising that the example of the Austro-Hungarian Empire, that was not a nation and barely a state, seems to him interesting to ponder for today's Europeans, who will probably have to get used to the idea of progressively outgrowing the frame of the nation state for the benefit of a type of organization above and beyond the state and the nation. Personally, I am not certain that the model of Kakania, from this point of view, is very applicable or its example very promising. But the important point is that the great twilight figures most typical of the declining Kakania, among whom we can count Wittgenstein, denounced it as also being the State in which hypocrisy and dishonesty, double standards, double-speak and double lives, half measures and conventional half-truths triumphed. And they reacted to this by advocating an exigency of radical clarity, sincerity and purity. As far as the problem that interests us is concerned, it is clear that a man like Wittgenstein could have no real sympathy for the behaviour of a society and of a culture whose entire program seemed to be, in this as well, not to choose and to succeed in remaining in a way in balance between the past and the future. For him, that is precisely the thing we cannot do and that we must above all not try to do.

Progress as the form of contemporary civilization

The two editors who published the conversations of Wittgenstein and Bouwsma write, in their preface, about the exchanges the two had:

While the two men are having a dish of ice cream, Wittgenstein reflects on how different this world is from the world of his parents — how the machines would have made our lives unrecognizable to them. He describes having heard John Dewey give a lecture on the kind of human being education should produce, and remarks: 'But I was a human being which was fitted into the old environment.' This remark captures something important about Wittgenstein's difference. He has, in a certain sense, a conservative mind. He is not at all impressed by the technological advances and scientific outlook of the twentieth century. He disdains the idea of moral progress in history and the notion that the world is a better place to live than it ever used to be. He is sceptical of the future of mankind. He attends to the detail of specific human beings' lives and does not meddle in mankind or in popular movements. He is attracted to Kierkegaard and Dostoevsky, both of whom share and develop these thoughts.[13]

When we consider Kraus's case, we realize at a glance that what exasperates him is less the idea of progress itself than the forms of idolatry it elicits and the kind of hysteria that technology's achievements or the accomplishment of feats of prowess, like the conquest of the North Pole, unleash in the newspapers of the period. The idea of progress, as it is currently applied, is no longer, according to him, a philosophical idea and has been transformed into a journalistic concept. 'Each parasite of the times has retained the pride of being a contemporary. (...) For it is the business of idealism to console itself for the loss of the old with the fact that one can gape at something new. And if the world succumbs to its end, then man's feeling of superiority triumphs as the expectation of a play that only contemporaries can get in to see.'[14] Regarding Wittgenstein, one might say that, particularly in his *Remarks on Frazer's 'Golden Bough'*, he also treats the feeling of superiority with which contemporary man regards his predecessors with total contempt, and that he is not at all impressed by the performance and the spectacle that the reality of what we call progress is today more and more reduced to. He is interested in and even passionate about technology, in and of itself, but he is not an admirer of the wonders it creates or of the benefits that it is supposed to bring to humanity. Even if the improvement of the living conditions of human beings can seem, at least from a material standpoint, to constitute the most tangible and least questionable aspect of progress, he nonetheless doesn't seem to grant much more meaning to the idea that we really live better today than in the past, a point where he is no doubt closer to what popular wisdom has always thought, or in any case suspected, than to the discourse of intellectuals. He seems, perhaps in part under the influence of Spengler, more interested in the particulars of humanity and in their concrete forms of life than in the idea of humanity in general and of its supposed progress. And finally, he is opposed to the idea, that Kraus terms paranoid, of claiming and completely subjecting nature in all its elements and all its aspects, an idea that, in the eyes of many of our contemporaries, constitutes the long-term plan that human beings should strive by all means to realize, and that is identified in their minds with progress itself.

The attitude of the conqueror and of the proprietor that contemporary man has assumed with regard to nature does not meet with any sympathy from him. On the contrary, he advocates a form of humility and respect in the face of the phenomena of nature and of the natural order, and even, if we refer to what he says in the *Remarks on Frazer's 'The Golden Bough'*, what we might call a form of 'natural piety'. Considering how mind-sets and behaviours with regard to this matter already started to evolve some time ago, that at least is a point which entitles us to think that there is nothing conservative about his position, and even that it is thoroughly progressive. Wittgenstein seems to belong with those who think, to my mind justifiably, that the problem of what we call the damages of progress will not be solved through minor corrections introduced step by step, but only through a radical change in attitude, something that, unfortunately, has perhaps been impossible for some time already, and that would consist in imposing upon ourselves once and for all a form of wisdom and moderation, sufficiently rigorous, resolved and effective, in the management of natural resources and in our relationship with nature in general.

The 'modern myth of progress'

The brunt of von Wright's critique is obviously not, as has been charged, progress itself, but rather what he calls 'the myth of progress'. It is a relatively recent belief that is a fundamental component of what we can call classical modernity. The most characteristic aspect of this modernity's representation of the future of humanity was precisely the belief in progress. 'Not just temporary progress', von Wright specifically states, 'or progress contingent upon the lasting good will of men, but progress unbounded and everlasting, progress as something natural and necessary. This is a new conception in the history of ideas. I shall call it the Modern Myth of Progress' (*TK*, 205). What is new in this idea is not the belief that humanity can indeed progress in various ways, but the conviction that the possibility and even the necessity of a progress that will know no limits are inscribed in the nature of human beings as a species. This is what leads Fontenelle, whom von Wright quotes, to declare that men will never degenerate, and there will be no end to the growth and development of human wisdom. Furthermore, as von Wright remarks, not only is the belief in unlimited progress — and to be more precise, the belief, that has been an essential constituent of it from the beginning, in progress through scientific education and technological innovations — based merely on a particularly feeble rationale. But also, we may seriously wonder whether the idea of unlimited progress, understood in such a way, is not liable to enter into contradiction at some point with the natural species itself, which necessarily implies an environment and living conditions which must also remain, at least to a certain extent, natural, and cannot be transformed in any way we could like and without any limits.

As von Wright states: 'the industrial form of production is grounded in technology, which is grounded in turn in the scientific knowledge of nature. In the final analysis, it thus emanates from man's rational disposition. If we are inclined to believe that reason has an intrinsic capacity to respect the biological conditions of man's existence on earth, we can then hope that an in-depth knowledge of these conditions will also have a regulatory effect on the forces that have final control over the management of industrial production' (*MP*, 163). However, it just so happens we have reached a stage where we must seriously question whether the exigencies of reason and the exigencies of the apparatuses it has created, the apparatus of production in particular, have not already begun to contradict the exigencies of the biology of our species. The idea that it might turn out to be necessary to impose limits even on that aspect of progress which, subjectively and objectively, is the most tangible and least debatable, that is to say the improvement of the living conditions and standard of living for human beings, is or should be something we should logically expect. As von Wright says:

One thing which power over nature can achieve is to increase the material well-being of men. Of this, industrial and technological developments give impressive evidence. There can be no question but that enhanced material well-being, standard of living, in many, perhaps most, cases is progress in a genuine sense of the word. This means that it is valued, by those who benefit from it, as an improvement of their lives. But it is not necessary that this valuation will persist when growth has reached above a certain level or when its repercussions on the environment or on the social order have to be taken into account. (*TK*, 220)

This is an idea that, contrary to what the defenders of progress believe or pretend to believe, is, of course, entirely compatible with the conviction that it is imperative and urgent seriously to improve the living conditions of millions of human beings who live miserably today.

We know that Wittgenstein never had any inclination toward the idea of progress as a constitutive and universal property of the human species. On the contrary, he considered it to be nothing more than a formal property constituting the dominant characteristic of a specific form of humanity and of a particular type of civilization. In the preliminary preface that he composed in 1930 for the *Philosophische Bemerkungen*, he writes:

Our civilization is characterized by the word 'progress'. Progress is its form rather than making progress be one of its features. Typically it constructs. It is occupied with building an ever more complicated structure. And even clarity is thought only as a means to this end, not as an end in itself. For me on the contrary clarity, perspicuity are valuable in themselves.[15]

In other words, the fact of progressing is not a material property that could be attributed among others to the civilization in which we live and the reality of which we could also wonder about. It is its very form, the form in which civilization apprehends all that it does, and if we ask what to progress means here, the answer is that to progress means to construct, and to construct in an ever more complicated manner.

As von Wright has emphasized, it is difficult not to perceive what Wittgenstein says here as an implicit response to another preface, that of Carnap's *Der logische Aufbau der Welt*, published in 1928. In it, the author alludes to the affinity between the spirit of the new philosophy — that of the Vienna Circle — and that manifested at the same time in the area of architecture:

We feel that there is an inner kinship between the attitude on which our philosophical work is founded and the intellectual attitude which presently manifests itself in entirely different walks of life; we feel this orientation in artistic movements, especially in architecture, and in movements which strive for meaningful forms of personal and collective life, of education, and of external organization in general. We feel all around us the same basic orientation, the same style of thinking and doing. It is an orientation which demands clarity everywhere, but which realizes that the fabric of life can never be quite comprehended. It makes us pay careful attention to details and at the same time recognizes the great lines which run through the whole. It is an orientation, which acknowledges the bonds that tie men together, but at the same time strives for free development of the individual. Our work is carried by the faith that this attitude will win the future.[16]

We may note that Carnap also asserts that in principle, the goal pursued in all cases is clarity, which means that the increasing complexity in the details goes hand in hand with research of an ever greater simplicity in the main outline. To which Wittgenstein responds that, contrary to what Carnap suggests, in this way of presenting things, clarity is not really the goal, but rather once again a means that has something else in sight. For the members of the Vienna Circle, the watchword is: clarify in order to construct or reconstruct. For Wittgenstein, as he emphasizes, the only question, for philosophy anyway, is to clarify, and nothing else, or, if you prefer, clarify to understand, 'understand' meaning here to clearly see the possibilities lined up one after the other. Which is a way of saying that there is indeed no real affinity between philosophy and the constructivist and progressivist approach manifested in a multitude of other areas Carnap tries to link philosophy with. Indeed, that approach has chosen to privilege and promote *one* determinate possibility.

'I vividly remember', writes von Wright, 'how Carnap's words moved me as a young student in Helsinki in the mid-1930s — and I think we were fortunate in my country to have received our inspiration in philosophy from a charismatic teacher, Eino Kaila, who saw himself in the vanguard of a radically new way of thinking' (*APF* 49, 49). Even though I myself did not read Carnap's book until much later, in the early sixties, I must admit that the impression the preface gave me was quite comparable to that described by von Wright, something that can no doubt be quite easily explained in a philosophical context outrageously dominated by the influence of philosophers such as Nietzsche and Heidegger and, more generally, by thinkers who, to say no more, expected nothing good to come from science and even less from scientific philosophy. Even today, I never reread passages like the one I quoted without feeling somewhat moved, perhaps because I am more sensitive than others to the kind of enthusiasm and romantic momentum that animates it and also because of everything that the message of Carnap and his friends can retrospectively represent for someone who has an inkling of the political and intellectual situation of Austria at the end of the twenties. If there is one thing one might regret, it is precisely that, contrary to the hope Carnap expressed, the future, the immediate future anyway, came in fact to belong not to the current that he represented, but rather to its most direct and most determined opponents. That is no doubt what explains, at least in part, the fact that I have never felt personally compelled to choose, in the way that it is most often done, between Wittgenstein and Carnap. And this, it seems to me, is one of the numerous points that allow me to consider myself quite close to von Wright.

Speaking of what he calls 'the mighty stream of analytic philosophy', he writes: 'In spite of the many tributaries which have, in the course of the years, emptied their waters into this river, I think it is right and illuminating to call analytic philosophy the mainstream of philosophic thinking in this century. In all its heterogeneity it retains the two features I already mentioned as typical of its origin: the emphasis on logic and the alignment with science. It is, in short, the philosophy most characteristic of a culture dominated by scientific rationality' (*APF* 49, 57). While this might seem surprising coming from a French philosopher, that is also what I have believed, if not from the very beginning, at least from the moment I discovered analytic philosophy. But that cannot be said without immediately compelling the observation that Wittgenstein was not an analytic philosopher in that sense. Indeed, he felt no sympathy for a civilization dominated, to the extent that ours is, by scientific rationality, and the last thing that concerned him was furnishing that civilization with the kind of philosophy that would have been liable to correspond to its intellectual orientation and to its deep tendencies. It is important to note in regards to this issue that, as von Wright says:

The thinking Wittgenstein calls metaphysical is stamped by the linguistic patterns and thought habits of a predominantly scientific civilization.

  The metaphysics which Wittgenstein is fighting is thus not one rooted in theology but one rooted in science. He is fighting the obscuring influence on thinking, not of the relics of a dead culture but of the habits of a living culture. (*APF* 49, 62).

In response to what philosophers like Carnap were trying to do, Wittgenstein once said that he was not interested in the idea of replacing a philosopher's metaphysics with a physicist's metaphysics. And von Wright is surely right to remark that philosophy can hardly get any more lost in the jungle of metaphysics, as he conceived it, than in certain recent expressions, most characteristic of a philosophical culture turned scientistic. But I do not believe such a situation could constitute a comfort for the metaphysics that are constructed in ignorance of and disdain for science and, at least apparently, in direct opposition to it. Wittgenstein obviously never believed that philosophy could attain a form of essential knowledge, different from that of science and superior to it. To believe in that kind of thing is again to give in to the temptation of aping the claims and imitating the approach of science in an area where science has no business. This is the kind of claim that Wittgenstein could respect in the great philosophers of the past, but he thought that what we have to do today as philosophers is quite simply something else.

Von Wright notes that he could give or could have given the great metaphysical systems of other times 'the respect and awe which he was disposed to feel towards *great* achievements in all spheres of human life' (*APF* 49, 63). It seems to me important to add that he was also quite able to feel this kind of respect for the kind of major commitment and investment that science represented, when considered as an intellectual enterprise and adventure. He certainly did not confuse science, considered in that way, with contemporary scientific and technological civilization, which he did not like. But he surely had no real admiration and not much sympathy for the manner in which science is practised today, linked to industry and sometimes even to war, for the scientists of our epoch or for the kind of philosophy they produce when they try to become philosophers.

Von Wright says of thinkers like Kierkegaard, Dostoevsky and Nietzsche, who in the course of the nineteenth century had clearly distanced themselves from the idea or the myth of progress:

The mood of these writers is not necessarily pessimistic. But it is a sombre mood of self-reflexion and questioning of dominant currents of their time, as they saw them. And these writers, we know, were more congenial to Wittgenstein than any nineteenth-century philosopher of the established style. From his early years he distanced himself from and condemned modernity in all its philistine manifestations. (*APF* 49, 50–51)

What must be also addressed above all in his case are the self-examination and the questioning of the dominant currents of the time. The opponents of progress didn't fail to propose numerous ways out of the dead-end path they think humanity has taken, the first of them being constituted by the suggestion that we should decide to interrupt, purely and simply, the process of emancipation that simultaneously liberated knowledge, morality and art from dependency on an external authority. To put it another way, taking up von Wright's terms: in one way or another to put knowledge back in the power of the Word, morality back in the jurisdiction of spiritual or social forces and art back under the obligation to entertain the public or celebrate the mighty people. Of course, in Wittgenstein, one finds no such suggestion and no explicit indication regarding some other route, which would no longer be that of science, of technology, of rationality and of progress at all, and that we should from now on endeavour to follow. Wittgenstein chose to live in outspoken opposition to his time. As von Wright says, he gave 'an example of "a changed mode of thought and life" which, if followed might provide a cure for what he thought of as a sick time' (*APF* 49, 64). But he did not propose that his time follow such a path and he did not think that whether the time followed it or not depended on what philosophers might say.

What can be done today for the cause of progress?

I would like to end this account with two remarks. The first has to do with the question of determining what name we can use to designate the phase we are now in. Are we better off speaking of 'postmodernity' or, as von Wright suggests, of 'late modernity'? I have elsewhere explained my position at length on what to think of and on what to expect most probably from postmodernity; and, like von Wright, I think there is not much of a connection between the attitude of the most typical postmodernists and thinkers like Kraus or Wittgenstein. The essential reason for this is that postmodernism is a doctrine which remains fundamentally optimistic and that does no questioning of the necessity, if not to progress, at least to move forward. I once even proposed defining it as the conception according to which we know less than ever where we are going, and we should above all not try to find out, but in any case we know it is important to get there as fast as possible.

   This looks exactly, or at least far too much, like what indeed ended up being the imperative of modernity itself. Von Wright notes: 'if Late Modernity is predominantly a sombre mood, the undercurrent in it which calls itself post-modern is predominantly hopeful. It sees modernity as something essentially overcome, transcended, and in post-modernity a beginning and a promise of a renewal in culture and forms of life' (*TK*, 226). Von Wright adds that 'a sceptic may prefer to see in the post-modern phenomena symptoms of the malaise of modernity rather than a cure for it' (*TK*, 226), and that is how he himself is inclined to see them. That is also exactly what I think and I believe it would be easy to show that Musil, for example, who had already masterfully described all the phenomena presented today as characteristics of postmodernity, perceived them, as far as he was concerned, not as signs that we are entering into a new era, but as symptoms of the hesitations and contradictions in which modernity itself has already been caught for some time, and which it cannot escape.

The second remark I would like to make has to do with the kind of help that criticism of progress can now provide for the cause of progress itself. Von Wright emphasizes that 'To abandon belief in progress as a historical necessity is not to abandon work for progress as a task' (*TK*, 227); but this task is today essentially critical. The belief in progress, when it takes on the aspect of a myth, is precisely what dispenses us most of the time from demanding and actualizing real progress. As Kraus would say, he who knows once and for all that he is living under the sign of progress need not ask if we progress, or verify that we do. One might indeed think that, strictly speaking, we shouldn't have to believe in progress: we should simply try if possible to make real and concrete progresses, in the areas where it is most important and urgent to do so. Instead of jumping around in one place, trying to believe and to make believe that we are advancing, we must indeed choose to prove there is movement by taking real steps. To put it another way, there is nothing paradoxical in considering that the belief in progress, in the form of what von Wright calls 'the modern myth of progress', could very well be setting itself up as one of the most serious obstacles posed to progress today. Von Wright's words should obviously not be understood as those of an enemy of progress, but rather as the words of someone who has understood better than others that progress also can be in need of defence, and perhaps pre-emptively against some of its current friends.

Translated by Francie Crebs, revised by James Helgeson

NOTES

1 English translation of the text of a lecture given at the Symposium in honour of G.H. von Wright (Institut Finlandais, Paris, 5–6 October 2001), under the title 'Le Mythe du progrès selon Wittgenstein et von Wright'. A French version of this text was published in the review *Mouvements*, 19 (January–February 2002), 126–41.

2 *Die Fackel* (The Torch) is the journal of which the Austrian writer and polemicist Karl Kraus (1874–1936) was initially the owner and editor, and then, starting in 1912, the sole author. All in all, 922 issues were published from 1899 to 1936.

3 'Der Fortschritt,' in Karl Kraus, *Schriften*, edited by Christian Wagenknecht (Frankfurt: Suhrkamp Verlag, 1987), vol. 2, 197, henceforward 'Der Fortschritt'.

4 Georg Henrik von Wright, *Le Mythe du progrès*, translated from the Swedish by Philippe Quesne (Paris : L'Arche Editeur, 2000), 12, henceforward *MP*.

5 Here, I have tried to find an acceptable English equivalent for the humorous place names 'Schmockwitz' (Schmuck's wit or joke) and 'Schweifwedel' (sycophancy, toadying). In Kraus' writing, the term 'Schmock,' taken from Gustav Freytag's play *The Journalists* (1853), refers to the character of the journalist who is mediocre, opportunistic, arrogant and corrupt. On this aspect and on Kraus in general, see J. Bouveresse, *Schmock ou le triomphe du journaliste, La grande bataille de Karl Kraus* (Paris: Seuil, 2001).

6 Victor Hugo, *Les Misérables*, translated by Isabel H. Hapgood (Madison, WI: Cricket House Books, 2009) (first publication of this translation, New York: T. Y Crowell and Co., 1887), vol. 5, 51.

7 Georg Henrik von Wright, 'The Myth of Progress,' in *The Tree of Knowledge* (Leiden/NewYork/Cologne: E. Brill, 1993), 210–11, henceforward *TK*.

8 Georg Christoph Lichtenberg, *Aphorismen*, selected and edited with a posface by Kurt Batt (Frankfurt: Insel Verlag, 1976), 219.

9 Robert Musil, 'Bücher und Literatur' (1926), in *Tagebücher, Aphorismen, Essays und Reden*, edited by Adolf Frisé (Hamburg: Rowohlt Verlag, 1955), 690.

10 See in particular 'Konservative Anthropologie: der Sohn Wittgenstein' ('Conservative Anthropology: the son of Wittgenstein') in Kristóf (J.C.) Nyíri, *Am Rande Europas. Studien zur österreichisch-ungarischen Philosophiegeschichte* (Vienna: Böhlau, 1988), ch. 4.

11 Georg Henrik von Wright, 'Wittgenstein and the Twentieth Century,' in *Acta Philosophica Fennica*, vol. 49 (1990), 47–67 (52–3), henceforward *APF* 49.

12 Compare for instance *Vermischte Bemerkungen*, edited by G.H. von Wright in cooperation with Heikki Nyman (Frankfurt: Suhrkamp, 1978), 14.

13 O.K. Bouwsma, *Wittgenstein, Conversations 1949–1951*, edited by J.L. Craft and Ronald E. Hustwit (Indianapolis: Hackett, 1986), xxiii–iv. Kierkegaard and Dostoevsky are taken here as critics of modernity, and especially of the rationalistic optimism that is constitutive of the modern project, which Wittgenstein looks on with the same irony and scepticism that they do. The same reasons partly explain his interest in Nietzsche's thought.

14 'Die Entdeckung des Nordpols' (The Discovery of the North Pole), *Die Fackel* 287 (1909), 13.

15 Ludwig Wittgenstein, *Culture and Value*, edited by G.H. von Wright in collaboration with Heikki Nyman, translated by Peter Winch (Oxford: Blackwell, 1980), 7.

16 Rudolf Carnap, *The Logical Structure of the World*, translated by Rolf A. George (London: Routledge and Kegan Paul, 1928/1967), xvii.

Pierre Hadot as a Reader of Wittgenstein

SANDRA LAUGIER

Abstract:
Pierre Hadot (1922–2010), professor of ancient philosophy at the Collège de France, published, in the late 1950s and early 1960s, some of the earliest work on Wittgenstein to appear in French. Hadot conceived of philosophy as an activity rather than a body of doctrines and found in Wittgenstein a fruitful point of departure for ethical reflection. Hadot's understanding of philosophy as a spiritual exercise — articulated through his reading of ancient philosophy but also the American transcendentalists Henry David Thoreau and Ralph Waldo Emerson — will find an echo in Wittgenstinian thinkers such as Stanley Cavell and Cora Diamond. Ultimately philosophy for Hadot is a call to personal and political transformation.

Keywords: Pierre Hadot, Wittgenstein, Henry David Thoreau, Ralph Waldo Emerson, Stanley Cavell, Cora Diamond, ethics, self-transformation

Pierre Hadot was not only one of the greatest specialists of ancient philosophy but among the first to introduce Wittgenstein's work in France, in two articles, published in 1959 and 1961.[1] And not by chance: Hadot's thought is intimately related to Wittgenstein's. Wittgenstein specialists have for the most part overlooked Hadot's work on the philosopher from the 1960s; conversely, Hadot could not appear in all his originality to readers who were unaware of Wittgenstein's philosophy. In later life, Hadot no longer spoke of Wittgenstein except by occasional allusions. However, in working out a general model of ancient philosophy as an ethics, a praxis of discourse and an activity of self-perfection, Hadot opened Wittgenstein interpretation to new, original readings, for example those of Stanley Cavell and Cora Diamond.[2] Fifty years after Hadot discovered and introduced Wittgenstein to France, the time has come to make manifest the radical relevance of his early work and the meaning of his

Paragraph 34.3 (2011): 322–337
DOI: 10.3366/para.2011.0028
© Edinburgh University Press
www.eupjournals.com/para

discovery of the limits of language and its ordinary character, indeed to show how Hadot's definition of *spiritual exercise* offers a new point of access to Wittgenstein and to the *perfectionist* dimension of his work. It will seem all the more surprising that — for many years until the recent republication of Hadot's texts on Wittgenstein — his interpretation was generally neglected, above all by Wittgenstein's eminent French commentator, Jacques Bouveresse (whether through a desire for primacy or a discomfort before Hadot's non-conformist reading style that made an analytic appropriation of the author impossible). The eclipse of Hadot's work sums up Wittgenstein's unclassifiable character as a limit figure for contemporary philosophy, as unavoidable for the analytical tradition as difficult to integrate within it.

Yet already in his first commentaries, in contrast to the more conformist reading of Gilles Gaston Granger[3] (in the sense of a conformity to the dominant Anglo-Saxon readings and to the semantics of the 1950s), Bouveresse was well aware of the difficulty of reconciling Wittgenstein's *perfectionist* moral tone to the framework of analytic philosophy. Although Bouveresse's readings have never corresponded with Hadot's, the former's work has emphasized aspects of Wittgenstein's thought not entirely reconcilable to analytic philosophy: the 'Austrian' elements, shall we say, simplifying, in the particular sense of cultural and linguistic aspects not translatable into impersonal discourse and international distribution. We will not comment on the lasting difficulty for Bouveresse — himself long *entre deux chaires* ('between two chairs'), as he joked in his inaugural lecture at the Collège de France — to embody simultaneously such a singular and critical author as Wittgenstein and the conformist analytical current that Bouveresse himself undertook, from the start, to advocate and represent in France. Nevertheless, Bouveresse's ability to understand the philosopher's tone and give an account of his ethical style, his particular moral and personal sympathy for Wittgenstein and his writing, shows his fellow feeling for a certain stylistic intensity that transforms radically our way of philosophizing.

Of course, according to Bouveresse at the end of the *Mythe de l'intériorité*, Wittgenstein's work leaves certain things as they were, teaching us to see them in a different way, in short, to pay attention. It is *perfectionist*, Cavell would say. Hadot would concur. Bouveresse adds, in the same vein:

For Wittgenstein would certainly have considered it as a complete failure if it had not provided, in the end, the most difficult things and not the simplest to those who have the will to think for themselves.[4]

What is perfectionism?

Let us start from the moment at the end of the *Timaeus* where we find a variety of *perfectionism*, one that, as Hadot's work has shown, is present in all of ancient philosophy:

These each one of us should follow, rectifying the revolutions within our head, which were distorted at our birth, by learning the harmonies and revolutions of the Universe, and thereby making the part that thinks like unto the object of its thought, in accordance with its original nature, and having achieved this likeness attain finally to that goal of life which is set before men by the gods as the most good both for the present and for the time to come. (90d)[5]

We employ here the term perfectionism, which Cavell proposes in defining the ethics of American transcendentalism. This is not such a far-fetched link, for Hadot was greatly interested in Thoreau and later Emerson. Cavell juxtaposes the classic passage from the *Timaeus* to a memorable moment in Emerson's essay 'Experience':

When I converse with a profound mind, or if at any time being alone I have good thoughts, I do not at once arrive at satisfactions, as when, being thirsty, I drink water, or go to the fire, being cold: no! but I am at first apprised of my vicinity to a new and excellent region of life. By persisting to read or to think, this region gives further sign of itself, as it were in flashes of light, in sudden discoveries of its profound beauty and repose.[6]

This is indeed a very striking point in 'Experience' for it is here that Emerson evokes the painful loss of his son Waldo. This effort — the desire in such a moment to approach this region, which he calls a bit later a 'new yet unapproachable America' — takes exactly the form of a spiritual exercise as Hadot defined it,[7] adducing as well the example of Marcus Aurelius in his *Inner Citadel*.[8]

This search for the best 'I' and for this other region associated with self-perfection is at the root of a morality that we will call, after Cavell, perfectionist. Cavell discovers it in discussing Emerson, although he traces its origins in Plato. According to Hadot in the opening chapter of the *Spiritual Exercises*, this morality existed until the Middle Ages, defining those spiritual exercises through which we cultivate ourselves. Hadot's move necessitates a new definition of spiritual exercise, in two senses: First, philosophical exercise is no longer, clearly, a 'tearing away from daily life', contrary to what is suggested in *Spiritual Exercises* (62). We know that by this 'tearing away', Hadot meant a fundamental dimension of philosophical choice: deciding to renounce 'social conventions' (*CI*, 190), to change one's way of living. For Hadot, as for Emerson, philosophy is founded on 'aversion to conformity'. The philosopher is a non-conformist (this is Emerson's definition in 'Self-Reliance', where the word conversion is already present). But in Hadot's search for a definition of stoicism and more generally of ancient philosophy the idea appears that philosophical change can be accomplished in daily life, through the understanding of the everyday, the down-to-earth (Hadot often quotes Kierkegaard), the ordinary (as Marcus Aurelius describes the beauties of ordinary life). The rehabilitation of daily existence is a new type of exercise, and ordinary language, as in Thoreau and Wittgenstein, is the new space of transformation-conversion demanded by philosophy.

Whence the second sense in which the idea of spiritual exercise is transformed: it is an exercise in *language*, a habitual and repeated practice and use of language: speech (the Socratic dialogue, seen by Hadot as a spiritual exercise); writing (considered as well such an exercise); and reading. In short, it is the privileged space of the ethical relationship to language.

The reading Hadot proposed of Wittgenstein in 1961 was deliberately ethical and perfectionist. Hadot was still almost unknown when he published a series of articles revealing the link between his conception of ancient philosophy as a practice and the therapeutic emphasis that he found, before his contemporaries, in Wittgenstein. Hadot was first interested in the *Tractatus Logico-Philosophicus*, and the silence which concludes this work. In a recent interview, he admitted:

It must be said that this end of the *Tractatus* is extremely puzzling. One can well understand, I think, why Wittgenstein attempted to bring his reader to the observation that all of his propositions are nonsensical (it is perhaps above all what he wants to do in the *Tractatus*). But if it is understandable, one still wonders why one must be silent. I make no pretence of elucidating this problem. Moreover, one doesn't dare talk about Wittgenstein after what Jacques Bouveresse has said. His book, *La rime et la raison*, is a true masterpiece that I admire greatly. I make no pretence of doing better.[9]

Hadot is the first, long before Diamond, to assimilate the question of nonsense to that of a 'silent ethics' contained in what the writer has not written. On this final silence, he writes:

Perhaps it takes its meaning in this perspective: a 1919 letter to Ludwig von Ficker, in which Wittgenstein suggests that there are two things in the *Tractatus*: what he said and what he did not say, adding that what he did not say is more important: 'my work is above all what I did not write'. Indeed, he says that what he did not write is primarily the ethical part. (*QE*, 134)

What Hadot finds in Wittgenstein is both the idea of a silent ethics, inscribed in the understanding of the limits of meaning, and that of a simple, naïve and ordinary relationship to the world, prefiguring Cavell's readings. Hadot places Wittgenstein, deliberately, in the tradition of ordinary language philosophy.

We know that Wittgenstein himself returned to philosophy after having called for silence at the end of the *Tractatus*. This poses the question of the relationship between practical wisdom and philosophy. Wittgenstein opposes the very existence of something like moral philosophy, since, for him, philosophy is not a theory or a body of doctrines but the clarification of our thoughts. Ethics would be more an activity, a way of living, than a set of theoretical propositions. Reading Wittgenstein allows Hadot progressively to broaden his ethical approach, not just to Antiquity but to the history of thought in general. In defending a model of spiritual exercise as 'independent of all theory', Hadot adopts a form of anti-theory occasionally defended by Wittgenstinians:

I realized that I had tried to propose a philosophical attitude independent, first, of any particular philosophy, and next, of all religion. Something that is self-justifying. (*QE*, 135)

Hadot's understanding and definition of spiritual exercise is of radical contemporary relevance in that it offers us a point of access to Wittgenstein's perfectionist dimension. The *Tractatus Logico-Philosophicus* first attracted Hadot's attention because of what it says about the status of language. For the *Tractatus* poses the question of language's limits. Many will insist — Hadot himself insisted — on the link between the reading of the *Tractatus* he suggested in 'Wittgenstein philosophe du langage' ('Wittgenstein: philosopher of language') and the mystical silence Wittgenstein proposes at the end of that work. This silence has, despite Hadot's lucid interpretation, inspired mysticizing readings in France and elsewhere. But the 'mysticism' of the *Tractatus* is not of a dreamed-of ineffable. The *Tractatus*'s silence radicalizes the question of language's, and the world's, limits, which cannot themselves be surpassed or even described.

Hadot recently made this clear:

In Wittgenstein, for example, what interested me, given the mind-set with which I read him in 1959, was above all the mysticism, or rather, for me, the mystical positivism. It was almost a contradiction in terms: why had Wittgenstein dared to speak of the mystical? (*QE*, 129)

Hadot thus corresponded with Elizabeth Anscombe, enquiring about the statement she attributed to Wittgenstein, that what was most important to him was a sense of wonder before the world. This attitude (which Hadot calls, elsewhere, the 'oceanic feeling') was difficultly compatible with the second Wittgenstein, who to Hadot seemed to have fallen into a kind of banality after a long period of silence. Yet Hadot was the first to enquire about the reflections of the *Tractatus* on the limits of language and its relationship to ordinary life. The Wittgenstein of the *Blue Book*, and of the *Investigations*, no longer attempts to clarify ordinary language (in the *Tractatus*, already, ordinary language was 'perfectly in order'), but, on the contrary, to follow it, to be guided by it. An undeniable link between the *Tractatus* and the *Investigations* is the immanence of language. It is nonsense to wish for an exterior view or approach. We are always inside 'a form of life' in language. Spiritual exercises are not a counter-example to, but a confirmation of, this immanence. They are always explicit, spoken: they are *language exercises*. This is why the idea of spiritual exercise is at least as close to the 'second' Wittgenstein as the first, and helps us understand the continuity between the two. In the *Investigations* as in the *Tractatus* there is the aim to de-sublimate philosophy, the desire to bring it down to earth (to 'bring the words home from their metaphysical to their ordinary use', *PI*, §116).[10] The continuity of Wittgenstein's work comes to the fore in this persistence of what is called, in the *Tractatus*, *Umgangsprache*, and in the *Investigations*, *unsere alltägliche Sprache*. For Wittgenstein and Hadot, language is always 'ours'; we are born in it. This is an ethical truth, difficult to accept: all our words are learned, belong to others, have already been said, and we cannot rise, except in illusion, above or outside inherited language. Language is our form of life, and there is no outside. This was said very clearly by Cavell:

[F]or those creatures for whom language is our form of life, those who are what [Emerson's] 'Experience' entitles 'victims of expressions' — mortals — language is everywhere we find ourselves, which means everywhere in philosophy.[11]

What we will call, after the great specialist of Hadot's work, Arnold Davidson, 'the spiritual exercises of philosophy', consists in accepting this destiny. The limits of language are those of our world and of my life: to recognize my form of life in language is to recognize my finitude. Spiritual exercises would consist, then, in understanding my situation in language. They are training for death and for the life whose

limits are those of my world. This is what defines the ethical sense of
the *Tractatus*:

> Thus, this silence can have a sceptical meaning according to the ancient meaning
> of the term. That is that it is a sceptical attitude consisting in living like everyone
> else but with total interior detachment, which implies the refusal of any value
> judgement. This represents a form of wisdom. (*QE*, 134)

This Wittgenstinian ethics defines a non-religious form of spiritual
exercise. In *Spiritual Exercises*, Hadot conceived of such exercises in
terms of the mastery of discourse (even interior discourse) and the
appropriation of a language game. For Hadot, the constant desire in
Wittgenstein's work is to abandon the will to emerge from language
and even (with more difficulty) that of theorizing the impossibility
of emerging. The abandoning takes place through Wittgenstinian
therapy, which does not heal us of philosophy but makes us understand
the nature of nonsense.

Language as Praxis

A second constant in Wittgenstein's work, also very characteristic
of Hadot's method, is the linking of language and praxis. This link
is already present in the classic, fruitful distinction between what is
said and what is *shown* in language. In the *Investigations*, Wittgenstein
affirms that what seems ineffable or incomprehensible is right there,
under our eyes, showing itself through words and through life. This
position is continuous with that of the *Tractatus*: language has no
outside, and to understand the author of the book (*TLP*, 6.54)[12] is
to understand that the book itself is meaningless. The unexpected
final insistence on the author in such a metaphysical work ('whoever
understands *me*') reveals the aim of the *Tractatus*, which is to transform
the reader, not to propose a theory: to transform her in getting her
to understand that what she reads is devoid of meaning and in what
way, not to tell her something. This brings this work, in its method,
curiously close to a certain technique of ancient philosophy as defined
by Hadot. The point of the work, for Wittgenstein, is not to produce a
theory of the world and a systematic discourse. It is, rather, to act upon
the reader (the interlocutor of the *Philosophical Investigations*, which
take the form of a dialogue). In this sense, as Hadot puts it in his
preface to the *Spiritual Exercises* in relationship to the *Tractatus*, reading
Wittgenstein would also be a variety of exercise. But every reading, as
Hadot progressively admits, is of this nature. It calls for transformation.

This changes the perspective on the analysis of language, which is no longer a question of discovering an authentic meaning for words: a myth that Wittgenstein dispensed with already in the *Blue Book*. There is no ostensive definition or original meaning. There are only other words. Language is there, before me. I cannot thereby return to the origins of thoughts. The words of those dead writers that we read today are alive only in the use that we have today for their thoughts. To look for their use is to bring philosophy to the level of the ordinary, not to reject ordinary language, improve it or analyse it, but to examine it to see if it perhaps contains answers — always already present — to the questions we ask.

The ethical sense of this return to ordinary language comes from the fact that language is thus seen as a point of access to the ordinary in our lives. Hadot is also offering a critique, central to his conception of ancient philosophy, of theoretical philosophy. Hadot adduces, citing Vauvenargues, the 'old truths' learned anew in each generation. Pessimism, melancholy before the world (the quiet desperation Thoreau evokes) are not contempt for ordinary life, just as in Marcus Aurelius the lucid description of physical and moral reality does not always entail disgust. The world is not the way it should be; on this everyone agrees. But it is only in this world that I can change. There is no other. This is what Stoicism defines, and its form of spiritual exercise (to change here and now, as by physical exercise).

It is true that Wittgenstein regularly discouraged his students from becoming philosophers, telling them to choose instead some 'decent work'. Hadot in the same spirit has commented extensively on the passage from Thoreau's *Walden* (chapter 3), where Thoreau asserts that 'there are nowadays professors of philosophy, but not philosophers'. We discover in *Walden* a type of ethics closer to ancient wisdom than to the puritan morality to which we sometimes associate American thinkers. Philosophy, for Thoreau and Wittgenstein, as for Hadot, is fundamentally practical. Thus, according to Hadot, philosophy in Antiquity is essentially reading and conversion. This type of conversion to ordinary life is very present in the variety of philosophical disquiet that we can hear in Thoreau, Kierkegaard and Wittgenstein. According to Hadot:

We can imagine the entire history of the West as a constantly renewed effort to perfect the techniques of 'conversion', that is, the techniques intended to transform human reality, either by bringing it back to its original essence (conversion-return) or by modifying it radically (conversion-transformation).

More, and better, than a theory of conversion, philosophy has always remained itself essentially an act of conversion. In all of its forms, philosophical conversion is a tearing-away, a breaking from daily life and the familiar. (*ES*, 175–6; 181–2)

Conversion would thus be, as Hadot's philosophy suggests, a return to daily life after this tearing away — but to a transformed life, 'a place where we have never been', as Cavell suggests. The things that we think ineffable or invisible are already uttered, are before us at our feet. We must simply learn to look: conversion is a turn of the glance. The limits of language are the limits of my world and of my life: to recognize my form of life in language is to recognize my finitude. This is precisely what defines the ethical sense of the *Tractatus*, as Hadot has recently made clear.

There is no ineffable; what is nonsense is purely and simply nonsense and cannot be thought. The rest can be thought and said. Ethics is not found in the ineffable, but in life itself. There is a good formulation of this point in Thoreau:

The at present unutterable things we may find somewhere uttered. These same questions that disturb and puzzle and confound us have in turn occurred to all the wise men; and each has answered them, according to his ability, by his words and his life. (*WCD*, 87–8)

Reading as Spiritual Exercise

Perhaps the tradition of philosophical spiritual exercises was rediscovered in those thinkers, Emerson and Thoreau, not well known in Europe, who inaugurated a tradition of thought later overwhelmed by the importation of European analytic philosophy in the twentieth century? It we have today become almost incapable of reading these philosophers in the terms proposed by Hadot, it is perhaps because of their misleading label 'transcendentalist' and because they have only been rediscovered recently, indeed through the emergence of a new reading of Wittgenstein. As the American commentators have remarked — notably Arnold Davidson — there is a relationship between the discovery of Thoreau and Emerson by Cavell and the rediscovery of ancient philosophy by Hadot. Hadot teaches us to read differently. More generally, he teaches us to read (this is the title of the last part of the opening chapter in *Spiritual Exercises*), and that (to parody one of his favourite expressions) to philosophize is to learn to read: that reading is perhaps the most difficult and most formative of spiritual exercises, very specifically in that it puts into the play the subjectivity of the reader *and the author.*

Far from devaluing writing as something dead, this philosophy of reading sees it as essentially alive. It is not enough to read, to read well: we must give, as Wittgenstein says, meaning, life to the words we say and read. From this point of view, reading is indissolubly linked with daily life. This is apparent particularly in Thoreau. To read *Walden* (as to write *Walden* at Walden) consists in opening our eyes, finding again the meaning of what we see every day, and regaining a lost intimacy with our ordinary existence.

To read well is to be reborn. Our words and our lives have lost their meaning and we must discover how to find that meaning again. This is certainly the (pedagogical) task that *Walden* undertakes, inseparable from its pessimistic diagnosis on our real ability to read. As Hadot puts it, elegantly:

> We spend our lives 'reading' but we no longer know how to read, that is to say to stop, to free ourselves of our cares, to return to ourselves, putting aside the search for subtlety and originality in order to meditate calmly, ruminating, letting the texts speak to us. (*ES*, 52)

We must recover lost contact with our own language, not to retrieve a mythical original meaning of words, but to arrive at precision in the expression that defines the ethics of language. This is indeed an apprenticeship and an exercise, an apprenticeship and an education: to learn is simply to continue to grow as an adult, which consists in, Cavell says, changing even when physical growth is over. Or even — since it is the mark of true change — to be reborn. It is this 'second birth' that the *father language* demands.

Language as politics

Speech and praxis are in Thoreau, as in Wittgenstein, intimately intertwined. Thoreau calls writing a 'handiwork'. Writing *Walden* is thus a way of making a living through one's hands, and a variety of redemption through writing. We don't lack for words or thoughts. It is not only philosophers who, as Marx said, have interpreted the world: it is everyone. All of us. It is for this reason that we must change, and act. It is the most difficult thing (what Wittgenstein called: *the bloody hard way*). Thoreau and Wittgenstein, and Hadot as a reader of ancient philosophy, inspire the same incomprehension, or difficulty, in what they demand of their reader: a reading as attentive and reserved as the writing of the original text: a redemption at the same time of language and of our life (of language by life, and inversely). It is in this return to praxis and this politics of language that we will be able to find as well the true meaning of the reading Hadot offers us of ancient philosophy.

It is not a matter of discovering the real meanings of words. There are only other words. Language is always there before me, there is no new beginning, no foundation. I cannot return to the origins of philosophy. It is too late. The greatness of Hadot's philosophy is to keep to this as a principle. The words of dead writers that we read today live only through the use we now have for their thoughts.

What is *native* to philosophy, at its root, is its ability to transform us. To philosophize is to learn to die, and to live; it is the same thing when we talk about learning. Hadot:

Since that time, this formula symbolizes for me both Montaigne's *Essays* and the soundings (*essais*) of my life, ancient philosophy and philosophy itself. I learned, then, still confusedly, but once and for all, that philosophy was not a theoretical, abstract construction, but an exercise, a process of learning, a training not just to die but to live in a certain way, in consciousness and lucidity, and that philosophical discourse only had meaning if it led to that result: in fact that this kind of philosophy was precisely philosophy as Antiquity had conceived and lived it.[13]

There is nothing new in Thoreau's text, no great discoveries to expect from the reading of *Walden*, and nevertheless this is a book that (in its apparent triviality) has the ability to change us. This question of change takes the form of a conversion. This personal matter is that of salvation: to earn one's living, one's life, is to settle one's accounts once and for all, but in order to do this, one must be able to work with one's hands. This is a salvation that cannot be accessed through morals, nor through philanthropy — strongly denounced by Thoreau and by Emerson — nor by philosophy as a theoretical activity. Whence the refusal of 'moralizing' morality that Hadot and Thoreau share: 'In a general way', says Hadot, 'I am not very moralizing and I fear that the word "ethics" might be too restrictive, unless it is understood in the sense of Spinoza's ethics'. The hypocrisy of morality in a narrow sense is constantly denounced by perfectionism, from Emerson to Nietzsche:

How long shall we sit in our porticos practising idle and musty virtues, which any work would make impertinent? As if one were to begin the day with long-suffering, and hire a man to hoe his potatoes; and in the afternoon go forth to practise Christian meekness and charity with goodness aforethought! (*WCD*, 259)

Philosophy, for Thoreau as for Hadot (as also for Kant, whom Hadot quotes at length in the *Inner Citadel*) is fundamentally practical. This makes the connection between philosophy and ordinary life at the same time obvious and difficult. Philosophers are strangers to the ordinary, to what Cavell calls the disturbing uncanniness of the ordinary. As Hadot says:

Already, Socrates in the Platonic dialogues was called *atopos*, which is to say unclassifiable. What makes him *atopos* is precisely the fact that he is a philo-sopher in the etymological sense of the word: a lover of wisdom. It is the love of this wisdom foreign to the world that makes the philosopher himself foreign to the world. (*ES*, 205)

But the philosopher cannot live elsewhere, outside of daily life (*ES*, 206). To take Hadot's reading method to its logical conclusion, we must understand that it is for philosophy to make a place for life, that is, in *becoming* ordinary, to surpass its classical tendency to wish to leave behind daily life.

This would imply reinventing philosophy (or rediscovering it). Is this still possible? Here again, only the beginning of an answer is possible. We might also think about Wittgenstein (who affirmed that if a real book of ethics could exist it would reduce everything else to silence). But Thoreau knows, better than Wittgenstein, that his book will only revolutionize those who wish to hear what he says, those who will see that the answer to the questions we ask is not far away. It is that — expression — which Thoreau sees as the solution to our 'lives of quiet desperation'.

The critique of conformism defines the condition of ordinary democratic morality. It does not concern only those who do not speak or who, for structural reasons, cannot speak: but those who *could speak*, and come up against the inadequacy of given words. It is in this inadequacy and this disagreement that the political subject is defined: not in a new founding of the subject through words, but in the smothering of and the demand for her own voice. The ideal of a political conversion — of democracy — would not be rational discussion, but the circulation of words where no one is insignificant, voiceless. This demand, this dissent are not excesses, they are not the edges and limits of democracy, but define the very nature of a true democratic conversion or of radical democracy. This tradition of dissent is rooted in the American tradition and has developed through many contemporary movements in America. Bercovitch has powerfully revealed the Emersonian origin of the tradition of dissent, distinguishing consent and disobedience: as if the initial dream of America could continue in internal dissent marked by individuality and by an American self-critique. We see thus the contemporary pertinence of self-confidence against conformism and democratic despair. The model of disobedience reappears against all of this despair: *not in our name*. This dispiriting character was already laid bare by Emerson and Thoreau as the impossibility of discovering another America as the emigrants forced from their countries had done: there is no longer a country to discover, no longer a frontier. 'This new yet unapproachable America' which we search for in the West, brings us back home. The dominating figure is not (as in Europe) the migrant, but the one who departs, the solitary voyager. The perennial presence in American culture of the figure of the errant traveller, the *sojourner*, is in fact the expression of radical individualism, of a freedom opposed to the State, not by organized revolt but by departure.

Emerson and Thoreau are indeed philosophers of *migration* and *atopia*, to articulate the problem in the schemas particular to Hadot. It is starting out that counts: always leaving again, not attachment, not rootedness, synonyms of the stationary, of *clutching*, of a tense grip on the nation or on the self. 'The most unhandsome part of our condition' says Emerson in *Experience*, is the moment when we seize hold of things: 'I take this evanescence and lubricity of all objects, which lets them slip through our fingers then when we clutch hardest, to be the most unhandsome part of our condition' (*CPW*, 103). Against the crepuscular vision of Europe's already completed history, transcendentalism demands departure. This is the meaning of Emerson's celebrated advocacy for the 'whim', for the caprice of departure, for example, Thoreau's move to Walden.

We can thereby, in this beginning that is the constant return of revolution, find our voice. We find again the meaning of politics; to find an adequate expression, to avoid these 'words which afflict us' since they sound false. 'Man is timid and apologetic; he is no longer upright, he does not dare say "I am", but quotes some saint or sage' (*CPW*, 21). This is also what makes Emerson inaccessible to nationalist or liberal ideologies, and makes him a true thinker of the everyday, of the ordinary) of the uncanniness of the ordinary. It remains for us to discover ourselves, and to make ourselves obscure to ourselves. About Thoreau, Cavell writes 'We have yet "to get our living together" (. . .), to be a totality, and to be one *community*. We are not settled, we have not clarified ourselves, our character, and the character of the nation, is not transparent to itself.'[14] The feeling of uncanniness that gives me my individuality is also a fantasy of inexpressiveness. We thus understand the meaning of the demand for voice; it is demanding myself that I can make my obscurity, my opacity to myself (*because* I give myself to be understood to others) become political.

We find here, again, scepticism in Emerson's construction of the new ordinary man. To make the private public, to make my private voice public: this is indeed the problem of democracy and of self-confidence. How can my individual and obscure *voice* be held in common, be representative. As, after Emerson and Thoreau each in their own way, Wittgenstein and Freud will say, we reveal ourselves in hiding, in the very difficulty of expression.

Because the breaking of such control is a constant purpose of the later Wittgenstein, his writing is deeply practical and negative, the way Freud's is. And like Freud's therapy, it wishes to prevent understanding that is unaccompanied by inner change. In both, such misfortune is betrayed in the incongruence between what is said and what is meant or expressed; in both the self is concealed in assertion and action and revealed in temptation and wish.[15]

Self-reliance is the requirement for the ability of everyone to find his own obscurity, to judge what is good for him or her. That is self-confidence: authority is centred on the ability of individuals (*selves*) each to follow their own capricious constitution. The political question becomes that of self-knowledge, in this sense — not a point of departure but of arrival, to constitute in my knowledge and in the ignorance of my being. We find here again the distinction between *I* and *we* from which we began. But this articulation, far from being rationalist as in many contemporary political theories, is sceptical. Dissent is not the dissolving of consent but strife over its content. In this sense of dissent, each is worth the same as the others, and every individual voice — fatality of expression and democracy — multiplicity. It is here and now that my consent to society is decided. I have not given it once and for all. One can find it difficult to accept such an individualist position. This radical individualism is, nevertheless, a possible way of access for the rediscovery of democracy not smothered under conformism. The paradoxical reproach that can be addressed to liberalism would thus take aim at its inability to honour individualist demands — as if in belonging to a society I had necessarily to give my agreement to it, give it as a rule, consent. Against conformity, Emerson and Thoreau demand a life that is ours, to which we have consented in our obscure, divided and individual voices. Thoreau:

I do not suppose that I have attained to obscurity, but I should be proud if no more fatal fault were found with my pages on this score than was found within the Walden ice.[16]

What these writers have in common, however distant they may be from each other geographically, historically and even (for all sorts of reasons) theoretically — is the desire to reinvent a status for language, to see language as both clear and obscure, public and private, ordinary and departing from the ordinary: signs are dead if they are not integrated in our (form of) life. The only thing that is unsayable is that which we do not wish to say, or read. When Thoreau evokes 'the at present unutterable things' which will be 'somewhere uttered', he designates (like Wittgenstein when he speaks of the limits of language in the *Tractatus*) what is there, under our eyes, the words that he is in the process of writing, his own text. This paradoxical position of the author is what makes the true experience of reading a text possible. We must *learn to read* these things 'already said' in order to be able to think and say them ourselves. It is this *art of reading* that defines, from antiquity to the twenty-first century, another history of subjectivity. This is not the least of the contributions of Pierre Hadot's philosophy.

Translated by James Helgeson

NOTES

1 Texts reprinted with other studies on Wittgenstein in Pierre Hadot, *Wittgenstein et les limites du langage* (Paris: Vrin, 2004), henceforward *WLL*.
2 Stanley Cavell, *The Claim of Reason* (Oxford: Oxford University Press, 1979); Cora Diamond, *The Realistic Spirit: Wittgenstein, Philosophy and the Mind* (Cambridge, MA: MIT Press, 1991).
3 See, for example, Gilles Gaston Granger, 'L'Argumentation du *Tractatus*: Systèmes philosophiques et métastructures' in *Etudes sur l'histoire de la philosophie en homage à Martial Guéroult* (Paris: Librairie Fischbacher, 1964) 139–54.
4 Jacques Bouveresse, *Le Mythe de l'intériorité: Expérience, signification et langage privé chez Wittgenstein* (Paris: Minuit, 1976), 674.
5 Plato. *Plato in Twelve Volumes*. Vol. 9 translated by W.R.M. Lamb (Cambridge, MA: Harvard University Press; London: William Heinemann Ltd, 1925). Text retrieved electronically from the Perseus project (http://www. perseus.tufts.edu), consulted 12 July 2011, 3:50 a.m.

6   Ralph Waldo Emerson, *The Complete Prose Works* (London: Ward, Lock and Co., 1891), 109, henceforward *CPW*.

7   Pierre Hadot, *Exercices spirituels et philosophie antique* (Paris: Albin Michel, 2002), henceforward *ES*.

8   Pierre Hadot, *La Citadelle intérieure. Introduction aux Pensées de Marc Aurèle* (Paris: Fayard, 1991), henceforward *CI*.

9   Pierre Hadot, Sandra Laugier, Arnold Davidson, 'Qu'est-ce que l'éthique?' Interview with Pierre Hadot, *Cités* 1:5 (2001), 134, henceforward *QE*.

10 Ludwig Wittgenstein, *Philosophical Investigations*, translated by G.E.M. Anscombe, 3rd edition (Oxford: Oxford University Press, 2001), henceforward *PI*.

11 Stanley Cavell, *This New Yet Unapproachable America* (Albuquerque: Living Batch Press, 1989), 117–18.

12 Ludwig Wittgenstein, *Tractatus Logico-Philosophicus* (London: Routledge and Kegan Paul, 1955), henceforward *TLP*.

13 This passage appears in Pierre Hadot's contribution, as Chair of History of Helenistic and Roman Thought, to the collective publication, *La Bibliothèque imaginaire du Collège de France: trente-cinq professeurs du Collège de France parlent des livres qui ont fait d'eux ce qu'ils sont* (Paris: Le Monde, 1990), 121.

14 Stanley Cavell, *The Senses of Walden* (Chicago: University of Chicago Press, 1992), 79.

15 Stanley Cavell, *Must We Mean What We Say* (Cambridge: Cambridge University Press, 1969, reissued 2002), 72.

16 Henry David Thoreau, *Walden and Civil Disobedience* (New York: Barnes and Noble, 2005), 254.

What Cannot Be Said: Notes on Early French Wittgenstein Reception

James Helgeson

Abstract:
Although Wittgenstein's philosophy long went untranslated in France, he was not entirely unread. Yet the relatively minor impact of Wittgenstein in mid-century French-language philosophy stands in marked contrast to the centrality of Wittgenstinian themes in Anglo-American thinking. Early French writings on Wittgenstein, as well a colloquium on analytic philosophy held at Royaumont in 1958, are discussed, and explanations proposed for Wittgenstein's limited reception in France in the five decades following the publication of the *Tractatus* in 1921/22. Possible effects of Wittgenstein's quasi-absence from French discussion in the period on more recent theoretical reflection are briefly examined. It is suggested that Oxford philosophers of the 1950s, and in particular J.L. Austin, had a more immediate impact on French readers.

Keywords: Wittgenstein, analytic philosophy, continental philosophy, Jean Wahl, Pierre Hadot, Pierre Klossowski, Jacques Derrida

> As far as Wittgenstein is concerned, I will set him aside, because after affirming that one must be silent about what one cannot say, he himself continued to talk about it, as Russell pointed out to him in his preface to the *Tractatus*.[1]
>
> Eric Weil, 26 January 1963

The structure of Stanislas Breton's 1959 *Situation de la philosophie contemporaine* is revealingly peculiar. Breton, a professor of philosophy in the Facultés Catholiques de Lyon, defines three principal currents of contemporary philosophy: 'existential philosophy', 'Marxism' and

Paragraph 34.3 (2011): 338–357
DOI: 10.3366/para.2011.0029
© Edinburgh University Press
www.eupjournals.com/para

'scientific philosophy'.[2] The first stems from Heidegger's influence, the second from Marx, Engels, Lenin and Stalin. The third is dominated by the Viennese circle and is associated with logical positivism.[3] Although Breton begins by distinguishing a trio of philosophical tendencies, the book contains only two chapters, and lacks one on 'scientific philosophy'.[4] Breton instead inserts into his introduction an extended overview of Wittgenstein's *Tractatus Logico-Philosophicus*, taken as representative of the 'scientific' strand (*SPC*, 32–45). Breton's overview of the *Tractatus* is detailed and not unsympathetic. Indeed, Wittgenstein is seen as being too 'intelligent' (43) to adhere entirely to the doctrines of the logical positivists. The discussion ends with a brief evocation of a link Breton sees between existential and logical philosophers. He writes of a struggle between 'rival brothers' (*frères ennemis*) who have forgotten their 'common origin' (45), which is, it seems, a reflection on the intentionality of concepts.

Breton's book was certainly not, even at the time, a major event in the history of French philosophy. It is, however, emblematic of the peripheral status Wittgenstein long held in French philosophical reflection, and so it will serve as a leitmotif here. Wittgenstein, who was for decades more or less unread in France, is a test case for historicizing the philosophical commitments of mid-century French philosophers and their consequences for later thinkers. Breton's account of the *Tractatus* is remarkable in that, when it was published, it was one of the very few texts in French on Wittgenstein, whose *Tractatus* had first been published thirty-eight years previously.[5] In an article on the reception of Wittgenstein in the 1930s, Jan Sebastik affirms that although the work found a public in England ('pays de grande tradition logique'), the situation was different on the continent: no-one paid, says Sebastik, much attention till the 1960s, until which time the *Tractatus* was a 'curiosité intellectuelle sans intérêt' (*LRW*, 197). To be sure, unless 'the continent' is taken to mean primarily French and German philosophers of a phenomenological or Marxist bent, Sebastik considerably overstates the case. The Vienna Circle of logical philosophers in the 1920s and 1930s must count as 'continental' by any measure, and in the circle's 1929 manifesto, three names are taken as representative of the 'scientific conception of the world': Einstein, Russell and Wittgenstein (*LRW*, 198).[6]

Still, Wittgenstein's French reception is striking because it is so limited, in particular if one compares it to the influence the *Tractatus* had not just on central European philosophers but in particular on their English-speaking colleagues. This influence was not confined to Europe and America: Chinese readers could study the work in their own language in 1927–28, some 34 years before their French counterparts.[7] Before the first publication of the *Tractatus* in French in 1961, the text had appeared in English (1922) Italian (1954), Spanish (1957) and Serbian-Croatian (1960).[8]

Despite the lack of a translation, the *Tractatus* did not go entirely unnoticed in French-language publications as early as the 1920s. The few reactions to Wittgenstein were respectful but sceptical. In a three-part article entitled 'Le raisonnement en termes de faits dans la logistique russellienne', from 1927–28, the Belgian logician Robert Feys refers often to Wittgenstein and what he calls his 'strange' book, the *Tractatus*.[9] The new tendency Feys identifies is Wittgenstein's critique and, in Feys' view, his radicalization of Russell and Whitehead's understanding of logic and mathematics.

In a 1935 *compte rendu* of the Prague Congress of 1934, and in particular the contributions of the Viennese logical positivists,[10] Jean Cavaillès speaks of Wittgenstein primarily as the instigator of the logical doctrines of the Vienna Circle. He begins with a brief, cogent account of aspects of the *Tractatus* (137–41), identifying three Wittgenstinian theses that he sees as inspiring the Viennese philosophers: (1) Language is the image of the world (137); (2) Purely logical propositions have no content: they are tautologies (139); (3) there are no propositions about propositions (140), that is, there is no metalanguage. Cavaillès is particularly interested in Rudolf Carnap's extensions of Wittgenstinian intuitions, which he sees as nuancing what he calls the 'overly mathematical notion of correspondence between mathematics and reality' (141). In the end, however, Cavaillès has reservations about the totalizing, or 'totalitarian' (*totalitaire* (149)) ambitions of scientific philosophy. He admires the clarity and precision of the Vienna Circle, but finds their work self-contained, doubting that it can be extended to other regions of thought: 'the discussions in Prague have brought to light the advantage of their clarity and precision: *they* are able to determine the true meaning and value of the results that *they* obtain' (148–9; emphasis in original).

After this, there is silence. Wittgenstein's *Tractatus* (the only philosophical book he published while alive) long went untranslated and unread in France. And logical positivism — with which Wittgenstein would be associated in French philosophical circles — had virtually no echo. It is striking that a search for 'positivisme logique' in the catalogue of the Bibliothèque nationale de France yields no results between 1937 and 1951.[11]

Breton did not write a separate chapter on 'scientific philosophy' since it is not clear what French philosophy might have corresponded to this name in 1959.[12] Nevertheless, there was more reception of Wittgenstein in the 1950s than Breton's brief overview, published at the end of the decade, would suggest. The Sorbonne philosopher Jean Wahl is a central figure in the story of post-war French Wittgenstein reception, a story that is revealing as well about the social organization of philosophical reflection in the 1950s. The delay in Wittgenstein reception means, however, that his thinking will long be inseparable in France from that of later British analytic philosophy, and particular the 'Oxford School'. There is certainly a new interest in Wittgenstein, but he will not become a canonical philosopher in France until much later.

In 1953, Ludwig Wittgenstein's *Philosophical Investigations* were published in Oxford, posthumously, in an edition edited by his students Elizabeth Anscombe and Rush Rhees.[13] The event passed without comment in France, at least in philosophical publications, until 1956. The first articles on Wittgenstein in French in the 1950s appear in foreign journals, in particularly in the Low Countries, and were by philosophers connected with Catholic university circles.[14] But by the mid-1950s there were stirrings of interest in France in Wittgenstein's philosophy. Emile Benveniste makes a very brief reference to Wittgenstein in an article published in 1954, entitled 'Tendences récentes de la linguistique générale'. Benveniste mentions Wittgenstein in conjunction with Russell, observing that linguists and logicians often talk at cross-purposes and 'logicians preoccupied by language do not always find interlocutors'.[15] He does not elaborate, and the passage suggests that the Wittgenstein he is considering is that of the *Tractatus*.

The earliest post-war articles on Wittgenstein in France were written by relatively young authors not well established in the Parisian philosophical scene. The first in-depth treatment in a French journal is that of Albert Shalom, who published in 1956–57 a two part review article entitled 'Y a-t-il du nouveau dans la philosophie anglaise ?' ('Anything new in English philosophy?').[16] Shalom, who was then in his early thirties, writes:

The philosophical situation in England is rather complex. In Oxford, discussions and teaching are undertaken which, at first glance, seem hardly related to philosophy (. . .) In the discussions between professors, and between students and professors, the *use* of such and such a word always seems to be in question, and the necessity of knowing precisely the subtleties (*finesses*) of everyday language. If the names of the history of philosophy are invoked, those that dominate are those of immediate precursors, Wittgenstein and Moore, and a distant precursor — Aristotle — and always in the framework of the analysis of terms. (653)

Wittgenstein — as will be typical of French writing in the 1950s, is here linked with contemporary British philosophy. Shalom — who had recently been in Britain and obtained there a copy of the as yet unpublished *Blue Book* — presents his readings of Wittgenstein perspicuously, in terms familiar to his French audience.[17] For example, in a 1958 article,[18] based on the *Blue Book* and the *Philosophical Investigations*, he writes of the problem of the reification of universals in Mallarméan terms: 'I have in front of me "a flower". In what sense can one say that this term is part of a language (*langage*) that, itself, represents a certain "form of life." This term "flower" refers to a real object, a concrete object, independent of me and of language' (488). Note the confusion between use and mention in Shalom's example. The reference to the symbolist poet remains implicit, and although Shalom's Wittgenstinian conclusions are not those of Mallarmé's mystical evocation of 'the absent of all flowers' in 'Crise de vers', the example is tuned, rhetorically, to its French audience.[19] Shalom expresses surprise about British philosophy's apparently ahistorical character; this will be a repeated theme in French discussions of Wittgenstein and more recent 'analytic' philosophy.

No doubt the most important document for understanding the status of Wittgenstein in the Parisian milieu of the late 1950s is a volume entitled *La Philosophie analytique*, containing the acts of a colloquium on analytic philosophy, over which Jean Wahl presided, that took place from 8–13 April 1958 at the abbey of Royaumont. Wahl, a slightly older contemporary of Wittgenstein, had been named professor at the Sorbonne in 1936. Wahl was Jewish and was interned at Drancy until 1942, but managed to escape to the US, where he was among the founders of the *Ecole Libre des Hautes Etudes.* He returned to his Sorbonne professorship after the war and was a major figure in the 1950s French philosophical scene.

Wahl was not unreceptive to Wittgenstein and analytic philosophy, a taste he perhaps picked up during his years in the US, although it was hardly his own philosophical style. The Royaumont colloquium which he oversaw was the fourth in what has since become a prestigious series, the first three having been dedicated to Pascal, Descartes and Husserl (this suggests that 'analytic philosophy' was, at least to some, of potentially equivalent and related interest to these canonical philosophers). Assuming that an international conference, with invitees from as far afield as America, would require some planning, especially long before email and commonplace transatlantic travel, we can date an intensified interest in analytic philosophy in Parisian circles from at least 1957.[20]

The colloquium brought together many of the major English-language philosophers of the day (Gilbert Ryle, P.F. Strawson, J.L. Austin and W.V.O. Quine, et al.) with major personalities in the French philosophical world, including Maurice Merleau-Ponty, Ferdinand Alquié and Lucien Goldmann. It was also particularly acrimonious and probably hardened opposition between French philosophers and their English-language counterparts. Gilbert Ryle is often incorrectly said to have responded to Merleau-Ponty's question 'is our program not the same?' with the disobliging 'I hope not'. This is, it seems, a misrepresentation.[21] It is not the case that the responsibility for ill-feeling can be laid solely at the feet of the English-language participants; if they do sometimes come across as peevish and insular, their continental interlocutors — see, for example, Joseph Maria Bocheński responding to W.V.O. Quine (184–5), or Herman Leo van Breda's responding to Austin, Ayer, Ryle and Quine ('many continentals have no real interest for your philosophy') (344–5) — do as well.

The most substantive discussions of Wittgenstein took place primarily in the context of the papers given by J.O. Urmson (on the history of analysis) and Gilbert Ryle (on phenomenology against the concept of mind).[22] It is clear that although the English-language philosophers are conversant with Wittgenstein (Ryle, in particular, has much to say about his philosophy), their continental interlocutors are not. Maurice Merleau-Ponty is perhaps an exception, although his remarks (93–5) are probably derived from the substance of the talk by Gilbert Ryle to which he is responding and not from Wittgenstein himself. It is difficult to tell from his comments in the volume how much Jean Wahl had engaged with Wittgenstein by the time of the Royaumont colloquium. Wahl had been a follower of Bergson in his youth, and compared Wittgenstein, somewhat counter-intuitively, to his former philosophical master (101).

Although the political sympathies of the French-speaking attendees are occasionally Marxist (for example Merleau-Ponty and Goldmann), it is noteworthy that major Communist intellectuals of the period — Jean-Paul Sartre and Jean Hyppolite, for example — were not present.

Many of the French-speaking philosophers invited to the Royaumont colloquium were not French. Several of these were Catholic clergy: van Breda and Bocheński (the former taught in Louvain, the latter in the Swiss Fribourg). Bocheński had fought against the Soviets in 1920 and remained fiercely anti-Communist; van Breda was a Husserl scholar who had saved Husserl's papers from the Nazis and brought them to Louvain, where they narrowly escaped destruction in the university library in 1940. Perhaps it is significant that Jean Wahl, Chaïm Perelman and Eric Weil were, like Wittgenstein and many of the philosophers of the Vienna circle, of Jewish origins. At any rate, the French-language contingent at the conference is more 'continental' than simply French. The conference took place under the aegis of a major establishment figure, and many of the scholars present are major personalities in 1950s philosophical life. Still, the relationship of the invitees to the mainstream of Franco-French philosophy — if this is defined as Marxism and existential phenomenology — is not always unproblematic and in some cases marginal. Moreover, the colloquium ultimately cannot be deemed a success if success is measured by good feeling, or increased contact, between philosophers on two sides of the channel or the Atlantic. Nor did it provide Francophone readers with a clear picture of the distinctions between Wittgenstein and more recent analytic philosophy, although it did show the diversity of the philosophical methods brought together under the label 'analytic'. The effect of the conference was, in any case, delayed as the volume was not published until 1962.

The distinction between Wittgenstein and more recent British philosophy will remain difficult to draw in subsequent years. For example, in a rather unsophisticated review from 1959 of the Oxford edition of the *Blue and Brown Books*, Gérard Deledalle writes:

If the contemporary English philosopher has trouble conceiving that philosophy might be something other than the analysis of language, the responsibility falls to Wittgenstein. The influence of the author of the *Tractatus Logico-Philosophicus* (1922) first exerted its effect through third parties. There was a time in England when the commentaries of Wittgenstein's Viennese disciples were preferred to the master's Heraclitean aphorisms. Then his Cambridge pupils — the same ones who so religiously copied out the *Blue Book* and the *Brown Book* — introduced everywhere — even as far as Oxford — the analytic method.[23]

Pierre Hadot's essays on Wittgenstein from the late 1950s and early 1960s have recently been republished (three of the essays are from 1959).[24] They are particular in that they are quite rigorously focussed on Wittgenstein's thought, and not the context of its production (Russell) or its influence (logical positivism and 1950s British philosophy). The slim volume also contains Hadot's reminiscences about his early philosophical life and about French Wittgenstein reception (or rather its quasi-absence) in the 1950s. In his introduction Hadot recounts how, in the early 1950s, he had become fascinated by Wittgenstein's linking of logic and mysticism, which apparently appealed to his own youthful religiosity; Hadot says that he had made his own (unpublished) translation of the *Tractatus* (8). He came to the attention of Jean Wahl, who, Hadot says, 'knew Wittgenstein's work very well'; Wahl asked him to give a talk on it in 1959 at the Collège philosophique that he directed (9).[25] This was a significant invitation for a young philosopher who was not a *normalien* and who was, at that time, still very much outside of the mainstream of Parisian philosophy. Hadot's reminiscences are revealing in what they say about the Parisian philosophical world, and the prestige of Wahl's milieu; he quotes M.-A. Lecourret, who writes that 'there was something *mondain* and snobbish in that College, an element of consecration as well, and some still regret that they were not discovered there' (9). Hadot's interpretations are exceptional in their acuity, as noted in a letter from 10 October 1959 from Elizabeth Anscombe to whom Hadot had sent an article on the *Tractatus*. (Anscombe responded with compliments and pointed criticisms.[26] Shalom did not have similar success with his British correspondents. He had a curt exchange in 1960 with Bertrand Russell — of whose dislike for Wittgenstein he was apparently unaware — concerning an article he had sent Russell on the *Tractatus*. Russell seems to have had neither the time nor the inclination to read it.[27])

On the whole, the philosophical novelties that the 'continentals' took away from their encounters with the Anglo-American philosophical tradition in the 1950s were not those of Wittgenstein's philosophy, but rather those of Oxford philosophy and particularly J.L. Austin.[28] Austin would have more immediate impact on French thinkers than Wittgenstein. In a famous essay, originally published in 1962, entitled 'Analytic philosophy and language', Benveniste presents an exposition of Austin's theory of speech acts, mentioning Wittgenstein only briefly at the beginning of the paper.[29] Austin's 'speech acts' will attract Jacques Derrida's attention as well, in his 1968 essay 'Signature, Event, Context', and later in a polemical exchange with John Searle.[30] The articles by Albert Shalom and Pierre Hadot would have no immediate impact, although Wittgenstein will remain an important intellectual reference point throughout Hadot's life. Shalom would spend most of his career in Canada, whereas Hadot would remain in France and eventually receive a professorship at the Collège de France, on the strength not of his work on Wittgenstein, which in 1982 was largely unknown, but rather his research in ancient philosophy.

When Stanislas Breton's overview of French philosophy, mentioned at the outset of this essay, was published in 1959, there was still no French text of either of Wittgenstein's two major works. The first translation of the *Philosophical Investigations*, by Pierre Klossowski, would not appear until 1961, coupled with the *Tractatus Logico-Philosophicus* (a publishing solution that Wittgenstein had himself endorsed in his preface to the *Investigations*).[31]

The translation could easily be blamed for the muted reception of Wittgenstein. There are many reasons it is not good: it is both inaccurate and in places incomplete,[32] moreover the polish of Klossowski's French often distorts the peculiarly oral character of some of Wittgenstein's remarks. Klossowski did not include a translator's note, or indeed any comment at all; Bertrand Russell's 1922 preface (by 1961 hardly the most up-to-date work on the *Tractatus*) was simply reprinted. Certainly a translation of such a lengthy and difficult *œuvre* as Wittgenstein's would have been a major event in most writers' lives. This seems not to have been the case for Klossowski, at least in the view of several commentators: Alain Arnaud neglects to mention the Wittgenstein translation in the chronology given in his book on Klossowski, and Ian James mentions Wittgenstein only twice, in passing, in his monograph on the philosopher's thought.[33] Perhaps the volume was simply a money-making proposition, which might go some distance towards explaining its imperfections.[34]

This said, the translation is no doubt somewhat better, or at least more interesting, than its reputation. Possibly Klossowski was not the happiest of choices of translator, but he was certainly a major intellectual in his own right. Both a writer and a visual artist, Klossowski seems to have supported himself from translation, in particular from German and Latin (he translated works by Virgil, Tertullian, Hölderlin, Nietzsche, Heidegger and others).[35] Moreover, Elizabeth Anscombe's judgement on what she read of Klossowski's work was positive. Anscombe was already aware, in October 1959, that a French publisher (she could not remember which one) had contracted for a French edition; she wrote Hadot that she had seen a sample of the translation, of which she writes that it was 'not free from error but (...) certainly a great deal better than the English. But that would not be difficult!' (*WLL*, 108). It is of course possible, but it is not necessarily the case, that she was simply being polite.

Contemporary reviews of Klossowski's translation were not positive, not negative, they were for the most part simply superficial. H. Bernard-Maître, for example, seems not to have read the volume. In the context of a general overview of works in the human sciences, Bernard-Maître gives a quick unsympathetic overview of the *Tractatus*, derived entirely from Bertrand Russell's introduction, followed by a quotation of the passage in Wittgenstein's preface to the *Investigations* where he speaks of the difficulty of putting his thoughts in order (this comprises the entire review).[36] Another reviewer ends his brief comment with the famous last sentence of Wittgenstein's *Tractatus*: 'We will thus limit ourselves to citing in its entirety the famous seventh and last chapter of the *Tractatus*: "Whereof one cannot speak, thereof one must be silent." '[37]

It would, however, be a mistake to suggest that the translation had no impact in 1960s France. Gilles Gaston Granger offers a rather structuralist reading of the *Tractatus* in 1964;[38] Gallimard seem to have found it useful to bring out a French version of the *Blue and Brown Books* in 1965.[39] The volume, translated by Guy Durand, has a sympathetic preface by Jean Wahl, who repeats his comparison to Bergson (10, 17), and in his closing gesture, reclaims Wittgenstein for philosophy:

In a form that is strange at first, ancient, eternal philosophy appears to us. We wish to operate on her to remove certain malformations; perhaps she will get better, perhaps she was not so ill as we first thought. And let us not forget that the doctor is a powerful mind, and, if we wish to speak in these terms, an important philosopher. (22–3)

By the end of the 1960s, a generation of Wittgenstinians had begun to emerge — in particular Claude Imbert and Jacques Bouveresse — of which some are still active today;[40] Pierre Bourdieu and Jean-François Lyotard first encountered Wittgenstein's thought during this period.[41] Still, in the 1960s, there was less Wittgenstinian influence than one might have expected among scholars working largely within the phenomenological/existential or Marxist traditions or within the emergent 'structuralism' often said to characterize French thought of the period.

If the translation cannot fully account for Wittgenstein's rather muted reception in the 1960s, we must turn elsewhere. Certainly one suspects that the lack of active familiarity with a field of philosophical references — broadly speaking, 'analytic' philosophy of language since Frege — made it difficult for early 1960s readers to make any sense of Wittgenstein. The dominant thinker underlying 1960s structuralism was Ferdinand de Sausurre, whose linguistic vocabulary is not easily reconciled with the post-Fregean logical tradition from which Wittgenstein emerged. Second, the highly fragmentary nature of Wittgenstein's *Investigations* could not easily be integrated into 1960s French philosophy which often had strongly systematic impulses, a philosophy that was, as well (like English-language philosophy) quite national in character, even though it was occupied primarily by a German-language canon. (This problem of divergent philosophical references is evident already in the discussions of the 1958 colloquium at Royaumont.) Third, Wittgenstein's philosophy seems to have appealed to readers of markedly theological, and not particularly Marxist, tastes. In addition to Pierre Hadot, several of Wittgenstein's readers in the 1950s, for example Pierre Klossowski and Maxime Chastaing, were deeply implicated in theological matters. At any rate, Wittgenstein was hardly a favourite philosopher of Communist intellectuals. Initially sympathetic to Soviet Communism, Wittgenstein had been to the Soviet Union in 1935 (the trip took place shortly before Wittgenstein's fellowship at Trinity College expired, and Wittgenstein had thought of settling in the USSR, although like Gide he returned disillusioned). It could hardly have been otherwise. Logical positivists and Marxists were both hostile to 'metaphysics', but the former would not easily have sympathised with a priori (metaphysical) theories about historical progression (however materialist these might be and notwithstanding the left-wing politics of many members of the Vienna Circle). If Tony Judt is right to assert that French intellectuals after 1944 were 'swept into the vortex of Communism',[42] then it is surely relevant that largely negative Communist attitudes towards Viennese logical positivism — a movement that Wittgenstein was thought to have inspired — would have influenced Wittgenstein reception, absent among the more engaged Communist writers of the period such as Jean-Paul Sartre.[43]

What are the results of Wittgenstein's non-reception? It is difficult, of course, to draw up a list of philosophers who did not *read* a certain author; how exactly would one know for certain that philosopher x did not read philosopher y, unless y lived after x's death. Marjorie Perloff has, however, drawn up a plausible list of major French-speaking intellectuals who were not *influenced* by Wittgenstein, affirming that 'Wittgenstein plays little role in the work of Jacques Derrida or Michel Foucault,[44] Maurice Blanchot or Roland Barthes, Julia Kristeva or Paul De Man.'[45] The affirmation should be nuanced, in particular as far as Maurice Blanchot is concerned, whose 1969 *L'Entretien infini* contains a chapter about Flaubert and Roussel entitled 'Le problème de Wittgenstein'. Alison James, in her article in this volume, has offered points of departure for thinking about Blanchot's rather superficial engagement with Wittgenstein, and so I will leave that question aside here. Perhaps the most striking example of Wittgenstein's non-reception in France is Jacques Derrida. It is very unclear whether Derrida had in fact read much Wittgenstein, even by the end of his life (anecdotal evidence suggests that he had not). In the *The Post Card: From Freud to Socrates and Beyond* (1980) we find the following entry:

May 1979. What cannot be said must above all not be silenced, but written. Myself, I am a man of speech, I have never had anything to write. When I have something to say I say it or say it to myself, basta. You are the only one to understand why it really was necessary that I write exactly the opposite, as concerns axiomatics, of what I desire, what I know my desire to be, in other words you: living speech, presence itself, proximity, the proper, the guard, etc. I have necessarily written upside down — and in order to surrender to Necessity.

and 'fort' de toi.

I must write you this (and at the typewriter where I am, sorry: sometimes I imagine an analysis, tomorrow, with a patient who would be writing on his knee and even, why not, typing; she, the psychoanalyst, would be behind and would raise her finger in silence in order to mark the beginning or the end of the session, punctuation, indentations [*alinéas*]).[46]

Derrida alludes here to Wittgenstein's most famous sentence, 'Whereof one cannot speak, thereof one must be silent' as a convenient starting point for exploring terrain familiar to readers of his own early philosophy: the opposition between speech and writing; the concern for varieties of articulation that escape presence in voice but which are characteristic of written communication ('the punctuation', 'the indentations'); the imperative and impossibility of 'presence itself' and even 'proximity', evoked through an ancient tradition of epistolary theory styling letters as intimate conversation. These are, of course, well known concerns of Derrida's philosophy from the 1960s, arising particularly from Derrida's early essay *La Voix et le phénomène*,[47] a critical reading of Husserl's phenomenology and especially his analysis of signs and indicators 'in the solitary life of the soul' (*im einsamen Seelenleben*) (22).

It would be interesting to know what Derrida's work of the 1960s would have looked like in the possible world where he had engaged with Wittgenstein in some depth. Caution is, however, necessary, when dealing with such counterfactuals. Moreover, Laurent Carraz, in *Wittgenstein et la déconstruction*, has critiqued a number of English-language critical works that attempt to draw a link between Wittgenstein and Derrida, including Henry Staten's 1984 *Wittgenstein and Derrida* and Newton Garver and Seung-Chong Lee's 1994 *Derrida and Wittgenstein*.[48] It is not difficult to sympathize with Carraz when, for example, he suggests that Henry Staten 'uses Wittgenstein (his name, his work, his thought) as a marketing ploy (*argument publicitaire*) in favour of the recognition by American philosophers and critics of Derrida's *philosophical* work'.[49] Arguments that suggest that Derrida is important because his thought resembles Wittgenstein's in some way, or conversely that Wittgenstein was important because he managed to think some vaguely Derridian thoughts before the fact, are hardly compelling. One must surely nod in agreement when Carraz points out that Wittgenstein and Derrida start off from different conceptions of the sign: Derrida's being derived from Saussure and Husserl, Wittgenstein from Frege and Russell (*WD*, 15). Yet when Carraz affirms, strongly, that Derrida's critique of Husserl's 'pure sphere of meaning' is quite simply not the same thing as Wittgenstein's 'private language argument' (*WD*, 35–6), one may by right have reservations.[50] The question of whether Derrida's critique of Husserl might have some similarity to Wittgenstein's 'private language argument' is not one the can be decided by fiat. The stakes are particularly high. This is not a small, local question of interpretation, as the influence of Derrida's early philosophy on the humanities can hardly be overstated. The variety of linguistic philosophy (post-Wittgenstinian and 'analytic' or post-phenomenological and 'post-structuralist') a critic chooses will have an immense impact on the types of arguments he or she sees fit to make about language. Such differences structure, I would argue, the debate between Searle and Derrida,[51] which many believe Derrida to have won, assuming that he has vanquished 'analytic' philosophy in the bargain and therefore dismissing a century of rich reflections on language without further ado. For this reason alone critical thinkers should be prepared to explore these two solitudes — shaped by the late reception of Wittgenstein and, ultimately, the lack of dialogue between philosophical traditions — of these putative *frères ennemis*.

NOTES

1   Eric Weil, from the discussion following his paper, given on 26 January 1963 to the *Société française de Philosophie,* entitled 'Philosophie et réalité', *Bulletin de la Société française de Philosophie* 56:4 (1963), 143. I have translated passages from French in the body of the essay, except for occasional short phrases. I am grateful to Joseph Pearson for his incisive comments on a draft of this article.

2   Stanislas Breton, *Situation de la philosophie contemporaine* (Paris: Emmanuel Vitte, 1959), 22, henceforward *SPC*.

3   Jean Wahl makes a similar distinction in his welcoming speech to the fourth Royaumont colloquium in 1958. Wahl also emphasizes, in what is perhaps simply a polite gesture, points of contact between analytical philosophy and phenomenology, *La Philosophie analytique*, Cahiers de Royaumont (Paris: Minuit, 1962), 9.

4   Breton underlines at the outset what he sees as the strongly ideological character of philosophical discussion: 'I shall try to define, in its broad outlines, today's philosophy, (...) to extract concepts that have become, sometimes debased, the slogans of today' (10).

5   See François Schmitz, 'Dédain pour le logicisme frégéen et incompréhension du *Tractatus* en France entre les deux guerres', in *La Réception de Wittgenstein*. Acta du colloque Wittgenstein (Collège International de Philosophie, June 1988), edited by Fernando Gil (Paris: Editions T.E.R, 1990), 175–96, henceforward *LRW*.

6   Jan Sebestik also speaks of the Czech reception of the *Tractatus* by Jan Patočka in the context of the Prague Congress of 1934, Jan Sebestik, 'Premières réactions continentales au *Tractatus*. (Jean Cavaillès, Jan Patočka)', *LRW*, 197–210.

7   François Schmitz briefly notes the existence of the Chinese translation, an after-effect of Bertrand Russell's stay as a visiting professor in Beijing in 1920–21 during which time he introduced current work on logic and mathematics to Chinese students. (The *Tractatus* itself had yet to be published, although his students seem to have been already aware of Wittgenstein and asked him for information about the Austrian philosopher.) See Xu Yibao, 'Bertrand Russell and the Introduction of Mathematical Logic in China', *History and Philosophy of Logic* 24 (2003), 181–96. The translation (whose accuracy I am unable to judge) of the 1922 London text appeared in two

parts: 'Weitegengshitang mingli lun' (Wittgenstein on Logic), *Zhexue pinglun* ('The Philosophical Review'), 1927:1, 53–98; 1928:1, 31–80.

Russell himself writes about China in Chapter 10 of the first volume of his three-volume *The Autobiography of Bertrand Russell*, published most recently in one volume (London: Routledge, 1998), 357–84. Chapters 8 and 9 of the first volume discuss Russell's experiences during the First World War (Russell was dismissed from his post and later imprisoned for pacifist activities) and a trip to Russia in 1920. On Russell's life, see Ray Monk's *Bertrand Russell: The Spirit of Solitude* (London: Jonathan Cape, 1996) and *Bertrand Russell: The Ghost of Madness* (London: Jonathan Cape, 2000), as well as the introduction, by Nicholas Griffin, to *The Cambridge Companion to Bertrand Russell* (Cambridge: Cambridge University Press, 2003), 1–50, in particular 2–17.

 8 François Schmitz, 'Dédain pour le logicisme frégéen et incompréhension du *Tractatus* en France entre les deux guerres', 176. Italian translation of the *Tractatus Logico-Philosophicus* by G. C. M. Colombo (1954), reviewed by Robert Blanché in the *Revue Philosophique de la France et de l'étranger* 86 (1958), 521. Blanché regretted that there was no French translation of the *Tractatus*: 'it would be good to have an analogous work in French (it is distressing to note that the final bibliography, which claims to be exhaustive, contains no work in French, and with reason)'.

 9 Robert Feys, 'Le raisonnement en termes de faits dans la logistique russelienne', *Revue néo-scolastique de philosophie*, 29 (1927), 393–421; 30 (1928), 154–92, 257–74, 396. ('Livre étrange, d'une concision énigmatique, mais puissamment déduit, semble avoir poussé la tendance nouvelle à ses consequences extrêmes').

10 Jean Cavaillès, 'L'école de Vienne au congrès de Prague', *Revue de métaphysique et de morale*, 42:1 (January 1935), 137–49.

11 The 1951 entry has no title, but is by British Marxist philosopher Maurice Cornforth, with a preface by G. F. Aleksandrov. It is most likely a translation of Cornforth's *Science versus Idealism: in Defence of Philosophy against Positivism and Pragmatism* (London: Lawrence and Wishart, 1950).

12 For Breton, the influence of 'neo-positivism' has been limited to the 'Anglo-Saxon' countries, without the movement 'denying its Germanic roots' (*SPC*, 33).

13 Ludwig Wittgenstein, *Philosophical Investigations*, translated by Elizabeth Anscombe, edited by Elizabeth Anscombe and Rush Rhees (Oxford: Oxford University Press, 1953).

14 See the 1957 review by Albert Shalom in *Etudes Philosophiques* 12, 433. The *Philosophical Investigations* were again reviewed, along with the 1958 Oxford edition of the *Blue and Brown Books* of the *Tractatus*, by Gérard Deledalle, *Etudes Philosophiques* 14 (1959), 107–8. The *Investigations* had been reviewed

in Italy as early as 1954 by F. Barone (who had published a book in Italian on neo-positivism the previous year) and in Spanish in 1955 by A. Fabrat in the review *Pensamiento*. Meanwhile, the 1954 Italian text of the *Tractatus* was reviewed in the *Revue Internationale de Philosophie* 9 (1955), 439, by Léo Apostel (a Belgian philosopher with markedly 'analytic' sympathies, who would give a paper at the 1958 Royaumont colloquium on analytic philosophy). There is an overview article by H. Meyer, 'La philosophie de Ludwig Wittgenstein', in the *Algemeen Nederlands Tijdschrift voor Wijsbegeerte* 48 (1956), 44–53.

15 Emile Benveniste, 'Tendances récentes en linguistique génerale' in *Problèmes de linguistique générale*, 2 vols (Paris: Gallimard, 1966) I, 1, 13 ('les logiciens préoccupés du langage ne trouvent pas toujours à qui parler').

16 Louis Rougier's 1955 *Traité de la connaissance* (Paris: Gauthier-Villars, 1955) discusses the *Tractatus* briefly (see particularly 119–25). Rougier, oddly, does not refer to the work by name (or indeed to the revised edition published in 1922), writing that 'Le mystère de la nécessité *a priori* des propositions de la logique a été dévoilé dans le dernier numéro des *Annalen der Naturphilosophie* d'Ostwald, paru en 1921' (119). Albert Shalom, 'Y a-t-il du nouveau dans la philosophie anglaise ?', *Etudes philosophiques* 11 (1956), 653–4; 12 (1957), 47–63. (In French *l'Angleterre* is common as a synecdoche for the United Kingdom).

17 Although not the *only* influence: Albert Shalom suggests that J. L. Austin had thought that Wittgenstein had not added much to G.E. Moore (663, n. 2); in the continuation of his article he will affirm that 'Moore called upon language as a control method *(comme moyen de contrôle)*. But it is Wittgenstein who transformed this critical principle into a metaphysical principle' (52). Note that Shalom says that the *Philosophical Investigations* 'partially incorporate' the *Blue Book* (660, n. 3).

18 Albert Shalom, 'Wittgenstein, le langage et la philosophie', *Etudes philosophiques* 13 (1958), 486–94.

19 Shalom is not the only writer to connect Mallarmé and Wittgenstein. Alain Badiou, for example, has described the *Tractatus* as 'Rimbaud's "A Season in Hell" rewritten in the language of Mallarmé's "A Throw of the Dice"' (*L'Antiphilosophie de Wittgenstein* (Caen: Nous, 2009), 103).

20 The participants may not have been given much advance warning (the colloquium fell between UK terms). W.V.O. Quine writes in his memoirs:

> I was invited to the Colloque de Royaumont, an annual philosophical event north of Paris. I rearranged my teaching to cover the required week. It immediately followed Harvard's April recess, so I could be gone seventeen days. It was my sixth trip to Europe, my first by air, and my most casual. With my small suitcase I walked across Boston Common from my house to

the subway — five minutes — and in twenty minutes I was at the airport. (W.V.O Quine, *The Time of My Life* (Cambridge, MA: Bradford/MIT Press, 1985), 272–3)

Quine seems have enjoyed his stay in Paris; he was invited to dinner in the homes of Jean Wahl, Aimé Patri and Ferdinand Alquié. Quine, however, was not impressed by the quality of the translations of the papers and felt that it hindered communication, to the point that late in the conference he spoke for an extended period directly in French.

21   Leslie Beck mentions this anecdote in his one-page 'Avant-Propos' to *La Philosophie analytique* (7). Strikingly, the printed exchange does not support his account. The context of the offending remark is the answer to a question from Merleau-Ponty about whether he was still in agreement with Russell and Wittgenstein's theoretical program. Gilbert Ryle says, not unreasonably, that he was not, because the idea of being in complete agreement with anyone was deadly to philosophy (98).

22   Ryle muses at one point on whether there should be a 'leading' philosophy, asserting that analytic philosophers think not. His choice to use the word 'Führer' (68) at this point is in particularly bad taste when one considers that Husserl had been dismissed from his post in Freiburg for being Jewish.

23   Gérard Deledalle, *Etudes Philosophiques* 14 (1959), 107–8.

24   Pierre Hadot, *Wittgenstein et les limites du langage* (Paris: Vrin, 2004), henceforward *WLL*.

25   For more on Hadot's Wittgenstein, see Sandra Laugier's article in this volume.

26   Anscombe writes:

> I have read your article with great pleasure: it seemed to me to give an excellent popular account of the *Tractatus* and — if I may say so — to be both lucid and elegant. It has the unusual merit of presenting an account which seems to be derived purely from what Wittgenstein said and not from what Russell or the Vienna Circle philosophers held him to mean. It is probably the first serious article on Wittgenstein in France, and I am delighted that it should give so good an account. I think that it is no misfortune that you had not read my book.
>
> The following points seem to me to be wrong (. . .) (*WLL*,107)

27   In 1982, Shalom, then a professor at McMaster University in Canada, on the occasion of the discovery of a letter from Russell addressed to him had been asked to respond to 'Russell's shade'. In his letter he asserts that although little had been written about Wittgenstein in France in 1960, 'there was a good deal of interest in his work'. See Albert Shalom, 'Reply to Russell's letter of 16 May 1960', *Russell: The Journal of the Bertrand Russell Archives* 2:2 (1982), 45–51 (48).

28 But see Maxime Chastaing, 'Wittgenstein et les problèmes de la connaissance d'autrui', *Revue philosophique de la France et de l'Etranger* 86 (1961), 297–312. The article, very sympathetic to Wittgenstein, clearly shows the influence of Oxford ordinary language philosophy, and is playfully written in a format reminiscent of internal dialogues of the *Philosophical Investigations*. The author published another article, with the same title save the substitution of proper names, on Augustine the following year.

29 Emile Benveniste, *Problèmes de linguistique générale*, vol. 1 (Paris: Gallimard, 1966), 268. It should be noted that Benveniste is more eager than Austin himself to maintain a distinction between performatives and constatives. The essay was first published in *Les Etudes philosophiques* in 1963.

30 The relevant texts are contained in Jacques Derrida, *Limited Inc*, translated by Samuel Weber and Jeffrey Mehlman (Evanston, IL: Northwestern University Press, 1988).

31 Ludwig Wittgenstein, *Tractatus logico-philosophicus, suivi de Investigations philosophiques*, translated by Pierre Klossowski (Paris: Gallimard, 1961).

32 Elizabeth Rigal calls Klossowski's translation 'often faulty with occasional lacunae' in her preface to the recent collective retranslation of the *Philosophical Investigations*, Ludwig Wittgenstein, *Recherches philosophiques* (Paris: Gallimard, 2004), 7.

33 Alain Arnaud, *Pierre Klossowski* (Paris: Seuil, 1990), 181–91; Ian James, *Pierre Klossowski: The Persistence of a Name* (Oxford: Legenda, 2000), 3, 116.

34 On the choice of Klossowski as translator, further research would benefit from an examination of his correspondence (which has not been published) and Gallimard's records regarding the translation.

35 Ian James suggests that translation was Klossowski's 'principal source of income throughout his career' (3).

36 H. Bernard-Maître, *Revue de Synthèse* 85 (1964), 163–4.

37 Jean-Blaise Grize, *Revue de Théologie et de Philosophie* 11 (1961), 293–4.

38 See, for example, Gilles Gaston Granger, 'L'Argumentation du *Tractatus*: *Systèmes philosophiques et métastructures* in *Etudes sur l'histoire de la philosophie en hommage à Martial Guéroult* (Paris: Librairie Fischbacher, 1964), 139–54.

39 Ludwig Wittgenstein, *Le cahier bleu et le cahier brun* (Paris: Gallimard, 1965). At least one copy of this edition—at the BnF—incorrectly claims that it first appeared in 1951 in the 'Bibliothèque des idées'.

40 There was a major colloquium in Aix-en-Provence, *Wittgenstein et le problème d'une philosophie de la science*, to which both Claude Imbert and Jacques Bouveresse contributed. The acts were published in the *Revue internationale de philosophie*, 23 (1969), 151–378 and reprinted as *Wittgenstein et le problème d'une philosophie de la science* (Paris: Editions du CNRS, 1970). By 1970, Jacques Lacan is commenting on Wittgenstein in his seminar *L'envers de la psychanalyse*, in particular the seminar of 21 January 1970. Alain Badiou notes

this reference in his *L'Antiphilosophie de Wittgenstein* (Caen: Nous, 2009), 91. Jacques Lacan, *Seminaire XVII*, edited by Jacques-Alain Miller (Paris: Seuil, 1991).

41 On the influence of Wittgenstein on some of these writers see the special issue on Wittgenstein the journal *Europe*, 906 (2004).

42 Tony Judt, *Past Imperfect: French Intellectuals, 1944–1956* (Berkeley: University of California Press, 1992), 1.

43 See, for example, M. Cornforth's *Marxism and Linguistic philosophy* (London: Lawrence & Wishart; New York: International Publishers, 1965). Cornforth, whose exposition of linguistic philosophy is, it must be said, often remarkably clear, ultimately believes that it has brought about a situation in which 'philosophers have no purpose apart from debunking philosophy' (249). Linguistic philosophy is thus an expression of class ideology that should be overcome by Marxism (260–3).

44 James Miller writes: 'In "La vérité et les formes juridiques", a transcription of lectures delivered in Brazil in 1974, Foucault also explicitly credits his own idea of language as a "game" to unnamed "Anglo-American philosophers" (I am translating from an unpublished French transcript, p. 6). It is perhaps of some relevance here to recall that Foucault's friend Pierre Klossowski translated Wittgenstein's *Tractatus* into French. On the other hand, Hans Sluga, a professor of philosophy at Berkeley, an expert on Wittgenstein, and also a friend of Foucault, reports that Foucault in the course of their conversations freely admitted that he had never studied Wittgenstein's work closely — though he was eager to learn more about it (Sluga interview 28 September 1989)', James Miller, *The Passion of Michel Foucault* (Cambridge, MA: Harvard University Press, 1993), 416, n. 25.

45 Marjorie Perloff, *Wittgenstein's Ladder and the Strangeness of the Ordinary* (Chicago: University of Chicago Press, 1996), 12.

46 Jacques Derrida, *The Post Card : From Freud to Socrates and Beyond*, translated by Alan Bass (Chicago: University of Chicago Press, 1980), 194.

47 Jacques Derrida, *La Voix et le phénomène* (Paris: PUF, 1967).

48 Henry Staten, *Wittgenstein and Derrida* (Lincoln, NE: University of Nebraska Press, 1984); Newton Garver and Seung-Chong Lee, *Derrida and Wittgenstein* (Philadelphia: Temple University Press, 1994).

49 Laurent Carraz, *Wittgenstein et la déconstruction* (Lausanne : Editions Antipodes, 2000), 8–9 ; emphasis in the original. Henceforward *WD*. There are no references to Wittgenstein in Leonard Lawlor, *Derrida and Husserl: the Basic Problem of Phenomenology* (Bloomington: Indiana University Press, 2002).

50 See Garver and Lee, *Derrida and Wittgenstein*, ch. 3, 61–100, in particular 89–98. Garver and Lee write that 'Derrida's position, to the extent that he can be said to have a position, has important similarities to, as well as significant

differences from, that of the later Wittgenstein.' Their intriguing epigraph is from Iris Murdoch: 'Language is now a prime philosophical concept, whether thought of in a Wittgenstein (unsystematic, empriricist) or a Derrida (systematic, metaphysical) style' (*sic*) (v).

51 Jacques Derrida, *Limited Inc* (Evanston IL: Northwestern University Press, 1988).

At the Margins of Sense:
The Function of Paradox in Deleuze and Wittgenstein

Reidar A. Due

Abstract:

Gilles Deleuze famously expressed distaste for the philosophy of Ludwig Wittgenstein and his followers. The two thinkers are here seen as irreconcilable. The critique of false problems and the refutation of scepticism found in Wittgenstein have no resonance in Deleuze, who was a systematic metaphysical philosopher in the tradition of pre-Kantian rationalism. Pragmatic-sceptical self-limitation of thought's capabilities on the grounds of existing practice flies in the face of aesthetic experience. Moreover Deleuze explicitly upholds modern literature as a locus of philosophical innovation. The comparison between Deleuze and Wittgenstein is pursued in an examination of the questions of 'rule following', literary practice and semiotics. Deleuze was hostile to 'pragmatism', whereas Wittgenstein and his followers could often be described as pragmatists.

Keywords: Wittgenstein, Deleuze, metaphysics, pragmatism, foundationalism, rule-following, semiotics

An essential incompatibility

It would seem that there is no point of contact between the two philosophers Gilles Deleuze and Ludwig Wittgenstein.[1] There are many, stated and implicit, reasons for Wittgenstein's absence in Deleuze's large collection of philosophical and literary interlocutors. In the television interview he gave with his friend Claire Parnet, *L'Abécédaire*, Deleuze famously refers to Wittgenstinians as a

Paragraph 34.3 (2011): 358–370
DOI: 10.3366/para.2011.0030
© Edinburgh University Press
www.eupjournals.com/para

destructive philosophical school, but he does not elaborate further on what this destructiveness consists in or amounts to.[2]

Deleuze's interest in the philosophical themes presented by English or American writers of modern fiction, such as Fitzgerald or Lawrence, and his philosophical reading of Lewis Caroll in *The Logic of Sense*,[3] made these authors attractive to him in his ongoing search for a philosophical position that would lie outside of both common sense rationalism and Christian metaphysical idealism. The Austrian Ludwig Wittgenstein was adopted into the family of British and American philosophers for similar reasons of pointing to an attractive alternative to current philosophical conventions. His later philosophy has thus been explored as offering an escape from certain kinds of scientific or metaphysical rationalism: logical positivism, Cartesian philosophy of the subject, foundationalism in general.

Now Deleuze did not find, indeed *could not have found*, ideas or philosophical motives in Wittgenstein that could serve his own project. There are three principal reasons for this.

Wittgenstein's later philosophy is structured around an ambivalence between pragmatism and foundationalism. Kripke's interpretation of Wittgenstein's scepticism emphasises the foundationalist strand.[4] Cora Diamond's therapeutic Wittgenstein,[5] as well as the earlier Oxford Wittgenstein of Baker and Hacker,[6] is a pragmatist and an anti-foundationalist. Neither of these philosophical programmes, the search for ways of refuting scepticism, the endeavour to dissolve all philosophical questions as resulting from false problems or the elaboration of a transcendental pragmatism, have any resonance in Deleuze's philosophy.

Second, Deleuze is a systematic metaphysical philosopher in the tradition of pre-Kantian rationalism, the tradition of Spinoza, Leibniz and their ancient predecessors. Wittgenstein suggests in his later work that the very idea of metaphysical rationalism is based on an erroneous interpretation of what language means, and could mean. The attempt to construct *concepts* that are not grounded in the meaning of words as they are used within some already existing pragmatic context is doomed to fail, according to Wittgenstein, since only existing linguistic practice can provide meaning for the words we use, even if these words are apparently conceptual and abstract.

For Deleuze, any such pragmatic-sceptical self-limitation of thought's capabilities on the grounds of existing practice flies in the face of aesthetic experience. The revolutionary aspirations on behalf of language demonstrated by surrealist poetry and other avant-garde literary movements offer philosophy an insight that was only partly available to Greek philosophers — it may be hinted at in Empedocles and Heraclitus — it is the insight that human language as well as ordinary experience are limited by self-imposed norms of simplification.

Deleuze uses the very difficult and technically complex term 'representation' to sum up these norms. Under the spell of representation, thought never lives up to its potential, but poetic language may reveal a realm of thought that lies beyond representation — without thereby being a transcendent or mystical realm. It is merely a realm of what is thinkable but not representable.

A third, perhaps more interesting reason for the incompatibility of Deleuze and Wittgenstein — a reason that is interesting also in the context of this collection of papers — is of a literary nature. Deleuze explicitly upholds modern literature as a locus of philosophical innovation. Yet his own style is dry and anti-literary. It is sober, free of rhetorical flourishes, whether professorial or poetic.

Deleuze's works written with Guattari, *A Thousand Plateaus* especially, can be seen as works of philosophical literature, adopting a style that is close to that of American poets such as Allen Ginsberg,[7] but these joint works are very different in tone from Deleuze's own. When the collaboration with Guattari ceased and Deleuze wrote the two-volume treatise on cinema, his style returns to an academic dry concision in the first volume, whereas the second volume infuses the academic style with a meditative tone, motivated by the greater open-endedness of the subject matter, the time-image. Yet, stylistically both volumes remain inconspicuous. The texts by Deleuze that many would find most beautiful, his short book on Kant and his study of Bacon, derive their effect from mathematical principles of construction and a laconic, even austere, manner of exposition.

It would seem then that there is no possible contact or dialogue between the two philosophers Gilles Deleuze and Ludwig Wittgenstein. Deleuze showed in all the stages of his philosophy an interest in the concept of signs. In *The Logic of Sense* and in *A Thousand Plateaus*, he develops original theories of language. Yet none of these theories and concepts exercises a function that is in any way comparable to the role that the philosophy of language plays in Wittgenstein's thought. The central question of Wittgenstein's later philosophy, the question that divides the interpreters of his work into different schools, is the relationship evoked above between *pragmatism* and *foundationalism*: if the basis of mathematics, language and thought is a certain kind of 'rule-following', and if philosophy's aspiration to construct foundations beyond the practice of rule-following is an illness, then Wittgenstein presents a universal transcendental pragmatism (like Kant he both justifies existing epistemic practices and sanctions a condemnation of practices that are only apparently epistemic). On the other hand, the immense *ingenuity* with which he searches for justifications and — at the same time — demonstrates the failure of any such search presents a problem of scepticism and hence a more real problem of foundationalism than the pragmatic interpretation of his thought would suggest. Now, neither the transcendental pragmatism of Wittgenstein nor his foundationalist scepticism find any resonance in the philosophy of Deleuze who is a *speculative metaphysical* philosopher.

Deleuze *claims* the right for philosophy to bracket the Kantian epistemological injunction against metaphysics. For Deleuze metaphysics is an immediate given, in the way that sense data or mathematical reasoning are presented as given in British empiricism. Metaphysics is given in philosophy, according to Deleuze, in the form of *concepts*. These concepts contribute to the construction of philosophical systems. The status of a philosophical system is different from that of a scientific *theory* in that a system does not merely consist in a series of statements about a particular domain of reality. Concepts embody an applicability that cannot be hedged in by any prior definition of the theoretical domain they are determined to apply to.

Metaphysics is thus not a philosophical discipline that one would gain access to only after a preliminary epistemological exercise. Metaphysical concepts do not gain value only after having passed some epistemological test. It is rather the case that philosophy is in essence metaphysical. Hence, the raw material of philosophy is the concept since there is nothing that is given *to* or *within* philosophy that would be more basic or more immediate than the concept. This conception of philosophy that Deleuze and Guattari present in *What is Philosophy?*[8] is also practised in Deleuze's own philosophical treatises. The concept is theorized in his early book on Nietzsche, in *Difference and Repetition*[9] and in *The Logic of Sense* is a treatise on being, language and ethics written in parallel to *Difference and Repetition*, which is a treatise on being and thought.

The problem of language always presents itself within a speculative metaphysical context for Deleuze. Concepts and theories of language do not serve to question the legitimacy of that metaphysical context.

For Wittgenstein concepts are, on the other hand, words used outside of and beyond the legitimizing space of their original context of use within an existing linguistic practice. This is the main difference between the philosophy of language in Deleuze and the philosophy of Wittgenstein. All that I will go on to say will be said against this background.

Wittgenstein and Humour

Wittgenstein's sceptical search for ultimate justifications of rule-following employs a sophisticated rhetoric of paradox. Jokes, puzzles, thought experiments challenge the enquiring mind to step outside of its habitual frame of reference and conventions of thought. If we use the term paradox to describe this whole rhetorical practice, we can say that paradox in Wittgenstein's *Philosophical Investigations* serves to propel thought beyond the limits that it imposes on itself through its own habits of reasoning. This challenge is made in the name of reason all the same, in the name of a philosophical and sceptical reason. The nature of this philosophical reason is elusive in Wittgenstein, since it is difficult to judge the role of sceptical questioning in his text: is it driven by a search for ultimate foundations — a traditional rational philosophical enterprise — or is scepticism a kind of therapy or pedagogy offered for his readers to teach them the futility of any philosophical search for foundations? If one pays close attention to Wittgenstein's humour and literary style one finds in his paradoxes an explosive force that is quite far removed from the somewhat pedantic, puerile or merely conventional thought experiments that philosophers often present. This explosive force is embedded in a point of view that is, to be sure, unfailingly directed towards rule-following, everyday life, the ordinary. Yet the point of view itself, animated as it is by the explosive force of paradox, makes the ordinary extraordinary. I do not intend to suggest that Wittgenstein's paradoxes are like conceptual artworks, they are not simply aiming to instil in the reader a sense of displacement or alienation in relation to his or her own habits of thought. The purpose of paradox is always guided by the sceptical problem. If one looks more closely at paradox itself one finds that it presents a puzzle that enlarges the context of discourse. The argument or story does not simply move towards its conclusion, but a small break occurs and it is not immediately clear what context is required to give a solution to the puzzle.

Whereas a live metaphor opens a horizon of meaning that is not completely determined or settled, a paradox opens a context that is not immediately defined. This is interesting in relation to Wittgenstein's pragmatism. If rule-following is a self-sufficient and self-sustaining practice, how is it then dependent on context? Wittgenstein's aesthetic ascetic paradoxes stage stylized situations in which the dense web of social and linguistic interaction that we observe in daily life has been replaced by slightly absurd and certainly comical performances. When such an interaction occurs in daily life it is comic. I once entered a sandwich shop in England. A tall quiet man, without a word handed me a piece of paper on which was written the German word 'Lieblingsfarbe' (favourite colour). He then said: does this mean love? (*Liebe*=love). He had assumed that I was German and wanted to clarify the meaning of this word. The comic effect of the situation arose from a change in context: I didn't know the man, we were in a shop where one would normally exchange sandwiches for money, not linguistic information. The gesture of handing over a piece of paper with one word written on it as in a code, seemed a parody of a spy film. When everyday life appears staged in this way, the conventional context has been broken.

Wittgenstein as Writer

Wittgenstein is of course an Austrian writer as well as a philosopher. His preface to the *Tractatus* and his *Vermischte Bemerkungen*[10] are works of short prose that can be compared, for instance, to Canetti. Given the appropriation of Wittgenstein by the powerful school, or schools, of Analytic Philosophy, attempts to integrate considerations of style into a philosophical appreciation of his work would inevitably be situated in relation to the interpretative canon of that movement. The hermeneutically sophisticated approach of Glock grounded in the study of Wittgenstein's *Nachlass*, thus takes as its starting point questions concerning his manner of thinking, of elaborating problems, writing down solutions to a problem in a string of variations on the same theme.[11] The hermeneutic task of understanding this method of variation certainly takes aspects of Wittgenstein's mode of writing into consideration but the end-point of understanding is to explicate this method as a type of philosophical analysis, as in his recent book co-edited with John Hyman: *Wittgenstein and Analytical Philosophy*.

Wittgenstein's use of paradox in the *Philosophical Investigations* does not on the other hand seem entirely reducible to the schema of a method of variation in the service of analysis. Rather, Wittgenstein considers paradox as an instrument of thought that contains a certain force or violence in relation to common sense and philosophical convention. The paradox is a thought form that explodes in the field of received opinion and opens a field of something that remains to be thought, but that is not yet articulated as a precise problem. We can say, of course, that ultimately Wittgenstein hopes to formulate the puzzle identified by the paradox as a problem and then analyse the problem, but the textual moment of the paradox, its manifestation on the page is a literary phenomenon in its own right, resistant to what may or may not be the philosopher's own intentions. This literary moment does not only have the quality of provoking thought in a certain way, it is also intangible, self-contained, enveloped around its own humorous effect. It is very odd that Wittgenstein scholars have had so little to say about the relationship between his sense of humour and that of a near contemporary such as Kafka. Both stage scenarios of grotesque encounters that seem to rattle our most deeply held certainties and the beliefs that guide our everyday life. Of course, Kafka's style is objective as well as hyperbolical, lending to these grotesque encounters a forceful dramatic vivacity.[12] Wittgenstein's style of humour is obviously more understated and bemused. The grotesque is not dramatic but cerebral. His encounters are minimalistic rather than enlarged.

The suggestion of a comparison with Kafka is still helpful for differentiating Wittgenstein's paradoxes, and the humour they express, from the purely philosophical thought experiments presented at the opening of Kripke's book on Wittgenstein. I personally find it funny to imagine someone who thinks that all numbers above a certain size, when added, yield the result 57 (but I must also admit that I need to be in a somewhat nerdish mood to appreciate the hilarity of that idea). In other words, there are thought experiments that may well introduce puzzles and problems, indicate that there are areas of thought that have not yet been explored by philosophy, and thus coax the reader into a certain attitude of reflection and perhaps scepticism. But Wittgenstein's paradoxes do more than this. They are not merely instruments of reflection; their effect is not easily or immediately identifiable.

In the opening sections of the *Philosophical Investigations* we are often faced with the shadowy presence of a Stranger, an Intruder or Observer, someone unfamiliar with our ways, insisting on being shown what we mean, or inversely obtusely insisting on his own understanding of our practice. This figure never acquires a body and a name, yet his impact on the philosophical situations described in each aphorism is akin to that of an observer in Baudelaire's prose poems,[13] a figure whose strangeness serves to highlight the comic nature of normality. At this point there is of course a certain aesthetic resonance between Deleuze's admiration for Lewis Carroll and surrealism on the one hand and Wittgenstein's own poetic sensibility and sense of humour on the other.

Deleuze and Philosophy

It could here be tempting to pursue this parallel by comparing the status and function of puzzles in Wittgenstein to the philosophical theory of *problems* in Deleuze. There are several reasons why we might resist that temptation. First it is difficult to compare a theory and a practice. Wittgenstein does not propose a theory of puzzles, but demonstrates through the use of puzzles certain difficulties of thought that arise both within conventional philosophical methods and within common sense experience, difficulties that stem from a sort of anthropological instinct towards giving abstract names to features of linguistic practice that, in fact, do not possess an independent existence, in the mind or in the world.

Deleuze never exemplifies or practices his mathematically based theory of philosophical problems. He illustrates and invites us to illustrate what problems might be through examples from the history of philosophy — and as a historian of philosophy Deleuze is unparalleled: his readings are subtle, systematic, and conceptually concrete. As is well known, his technique is taken from his predecessors, Goldschmidt, Veuillemin, Guéroult, et al., historians who created an original French school of reconstructive history of philosophical systems. Deleuze's own thought never, on the other hand, proceeds through an exploration of problems. His method is constructive, he builds layer upon layer of philosophical theory encompassing a large variety of empirical and non-empirical domains, held up by the relationship between its central concepts.

Second, Deleuze views the vocation of thought as the discovery of new domains of thinkables or *things to think* and he sees this vocation embodied equally in the two creative practices that he draws inspiration from, surrealist literature and mathematics. There is, then, for Deleuze a *continuum* between literary, mathematical and

philosophical invention, between problems that we encounter in
literature and problems that emerge from a philosophical system. This
continuum presupposes that philosophy is rationally neutral, that is,
neutral with respect to the distinction between discourses that lay
claim to be rational and adhere to some specific rational norm of
justification and discourses that are indifferent to problems of rational
self-justification. This neutrality in Deleuze's philosophy runs very
deep and characterizes his entire enterprise. Wittgenstein, for all his
poetic sensibility and veneration for literature would not endorse such
a principle of neutrality, I think.

Third, language is never for Deleuze an instrument that self-
consciously aims at lucidity, clarification, analysis, simplification and
the like. Like the Stoics, Deleuze thinks of language as a particular kind
of *being*. To explore further the metaphysical incompatibility between
Wittgenstein and Deleuze we should look for a moment at Deleuze's
conception of language and signification.

Deleuze and Semiotics

Deleuze showed in all the stages of his philosophy an interest in the
concept of *signs*. In *The Logic of Sense* and in *Thousand Plateaus*, Deleuze
develops original theories of language as a type of being (*sense*) and as
a social activity.

In his early semiotics Deleuze follows the stoics and Hobbes in
thinking of signs universally as natural phenomena: anything can be a
sign for something else, the scar is a sign of the wound that it precedes,
the cloud is a sign of the rain that may come. This is the notion of signs
as a primary problematization that we find in the theory of perception
in *Difference and Repetition*.

The mind's most rudimentary and least abstract engagement with
the world consists in sensation (passive synthesis) and signifying
problematization (active synthesis). The sign is a feature of this active
synthesis, of the mind's interaction with its environment, a first step of
abstraction. The scar is not just a pattern, the cloud is not just a dot in
the sky, as signs they are more than just material objects, they carry a
temporal reference, hence a meaning — and meanings are not objects,
even when they are carried by objects.

In the Proust book[14] Deleuze argues that the novel describes a kind
of objective illusion that would permeate different areas of experience.
This illusion consists in believing (1) that the sign's meaning is an

object of possible experience; (2) that the sign is always fulfilled. In other words, signs are never just empty. They refer to something that could be experienced, by me or by you, in any case by someone. Signs are not just signifying the possibility of meaning but actually convey meaning. The most powerful examples of this illusion in the *Recherche* are to be found in the field of snobbery and of nostalgia. It takes Marcel a very long time to realize that the air of refinement and nobility that surrounds the Princesse de Guermantes does not correspond to any substantial human qualities, whether intellectual, emotional or moral. She is charming, but also cold, cruel and shallow — although she of course excels at masking these negative qualities. The signs that she emits are thus in a sense void, unfulfilled, and they do not refer to any absent object — such as inner depth, knowledge or emotional warmth that one could one day, with patience, discover.

An emblematic moment of disillusionment is enacted in a conversation between an ageing Marcel and the woman Gilberte that he was in love with as an adolescent. What is terrifying he says, is not the unrequited or unhappy love, but the love that dies away. What once mattered above all other things, the whereabouts of the beloved, her gestures and feelings, all of this suddenly ceases to carry any importance. In Deleuze's semiotic interpretation this disillusionment is the discovery that the signs that lovers produce and perceive are not inseparable from the emotional content that they apparently signify so directly: I may remember the gesture and yet be unable to relive the emotion.

The drift of Deleuze's early semiotics is thus a movement from nature towards an ideal realm of signs and signification. Signs are not just a product of society. Whenever the mind engages with its natural or social environment, it problematizes what it perceives in a signifying and temporal way. By so doing, the mind discovers that objects and actions exercise a signifying function that is not exactly identical with the object itself. The more one allows the signifying function to become autonomous in relation to the object that carries the sign the more one realizes that the realm of signification is separate from the domain of material existence.

In *The Logic of Sense* Deleuze explores further the idea that language has its own ideal mode of being. He calls this being 'sense' and suggests that sense is a transcendental, albeit existing, realm of meaning-possibility. It is a sort of precategorial genetic space where all the categorial divisions and distinctions between meaning that can be made in a language are mapped out. For this process of differentiation to be self-limiting it needs to possess a relation to that which is not meaning-full, i.e. to non-sense. In Deleuze's ontology of sense, non-sense is also a kind of being, is also, that is, real, but it is not figured plastically as a kind of space, but rather as a moving point.

From Sense to Non-Sense

In the course of *The Logic of Sense*, the moving point of non-sense gradually acquires the status of a strategic concept with which Deleuze proposes a dialectic of meaning and meaninglessness, sense and non-sense. This is quite straightforwardly Hegelian: in order for something to be what it is it must have borders, for the border to be drawn it must be conceivable *that* there is something on the other side of the border, and we must be able to conceive *what* this is. What is inside the border is negatively dependent on what is outside the border. It is what it is by not being what it is not. Yet non-sense does not simply determine sense in this somewhat crude dialectic of the border. The visual metaphors that Deleuze uses to specify the agency of non-sense do not suggest a movement of determination or constitution of identity.

This is because sense is not primarily word-meaning, possessing an identity in the manner of an essence or a phenomenological *noema*. The being of sense is itself a non-being — it has being but the quality of this being is a kind of non-being. This category is modelled on the Stoic sayable that is not entirely part of the causally determined order of the cosmos. Deleuze says that it subsists rather than exists.

Sense gains specification, becomes intentional, conceptual, referential meaning through a process of differentiation and for this process to be operative non-sense is required we are told — but why should this be so? This is so because non-sense is intrinsically *undetermined* and hence only defined in relation to sense, but the relation it has to sense is itself not fixed but constantly changing, since precisely non-sense itself does not have fixed limits. At each moment of the genesis of sense intention, concept, reference, the specification of sense has its ultimate limit in the limitless element of non-sense. Hence when I say love, or I love you, or you are beautiful or something of the kind my intention is carried into language by the possibility of saying UVIOL. UVIOL is of course a phonetic anagram of 'I love you' but it could also be an SMS saying: you are like a viol, hinting at Annie's character being similar to that musical instrument. The paradox is here a possibility that displays a genetic origin. The minimal possibility of sense is not identical with the fully-fledged, completed realization of sense within empirical communication.

Hence Deleuze searches for an origin of sense that is not identical with communication as it appears in everyday life, or as Husserl would say, in the *natural attitude*. The equivalent of a phenomenological reduction in Deleuze does not serve to lay bare a realm of constitution where the basic *entities* of thought acquire their essence, but to reveal a process of genetic constitution within language, a process that is alive within language-use as well as within its transcendental genetic possibility. In other words this is a genetic conception of language that sees the genetic process as being followed through into the existence of that which it generates and thereby constitutes.

This process is determined by non-sense paradoxes because only the possibility of irreducible self-reference, and non-sensical ambiguity, reveal that hard kernel of language in which sense has not yet become communication. Non-sense is that element of language in which it displays a nature prior to the concrete unfolding of language as everyday communication.

The parallel between the constitution of being as difference — as exposed in *Difference and Repetition* — and the constitution of sense through non-sense — in *The Logic of Sense* — lies in this search for a level of genetic constitution which is both transcendental and separated from the level of manifest existence — of being or of language since the things that are constituted do not 'look like' the genetic process — but which at the same time is *present* in actual being or language *as a genetic principle*.

In manifest empirical existence things appear within complex relationships, but these relationships may not be the key to understanding their origin. The level of constitution is not on the other hand simply arbitrarily different from the level of manifest existence. Rather it is organized around the primary element of being which is the self-differentiating genetic force from which the universe, and in parallel, thought and language acquire multiplicity.

NOTES

1   I have referred to Ludwig Wittgenstein, *Werke I* (Frankfurt: Suhrkamp, 1980) for the *Tractatus Logico-Philosophicus* and the *Philosophische Untersuchungen* (*Philosophical Investigations*).

2 DVD: Gilles Deleuze and Claire Parnet, *L'Abécédaire de Gilles Deleuze* (Paris: Editions Montparnasse-Regards, 2004).

3 Gilles Deleuze, *Logique du sens* (Paris: Minuit, 1969).

4 Saul A. Kripke, *Wittgenstein on Rules and Private Language* (Oxford: Blackwell, 1982).

5 Cora Diamond, *The Realistic Spirit* (Cambridge, MA: MIT Press, 1991).

6 G.P. Baker and P.M.S. Hacker, *Wittgenstein: Meaning and Understanding* (Oxford: Blackwell, 1992).

7 Allen Ginsberg, *Collected Poems 1947–1985* (Harmondsworth: Penguin, 1995).

8 Gilles Deleuze and Félix Guattari, *Qu'est-ce que la philosophie?* (Paris: Minuit, 1991).

9 Gilles Deleuze, *Différence et répétition* (Paris: PUF, 1968).

10 Ludwig Wittgenstein, *Vermischte Bemerkungen*, edited by Georg Henrik von Wright (Oxford: Blackwell, 1977).

11 See Robert L. Arrington and Hans-Johann Glock, *Wittgenstein's Philosophical Investigations* (Routledge: London, 1991) and Hans-Johann Glock and John Hyman, *Wittgenstein and Analytical Philosophy* (Oxford: Oxford University Press, 2009).

12 I have consulted Franz Kafka, *Sämtliche Erzählungen* (Frankfurt: Fischer, 1972).

13 I have referred to Charles Baudelaire, *Oeuvres complètes*, edited by Claude Pinchois, 2 vols (Paris: Gallimard, Editions de la Pléiade, 1964).

14 Gilles Deleuze, *Proust et les signes* (Paris: PUF, 1976.) See Marcel Proust, *A la recherche du temps perdu* (Paris: Gallimard, Editions de la Pléiade, 1988–90).

Skinner, Wittgenstein and Historical Method

Jonathan Havercroft

Abstract:

In a recent criticism of Quentin Skinner's historical method Peter Steinberger has drawn upon linguistic analytic philosophy to argue that intellectual history should focus on the reconstruction of logical propositions rather than the contextualization of author's statements. This essay will argue that Steinberger reproduces many of the same types of methodological problems that prompted Skinner's initial critique of intellectual history in the 1960s. I will draw upon the linguistic philosophy of Ludwig Wittgenstein to demonstrate that Steinberger's conception of intellectual history as the reconstruction of the logical content of statements fundamentally misunderstands what political philosophy is – and by extension the methods of historical interpretation.

Keywords: Wittgenstein, Quentin Skinner, historical method, interpretation, speech acts, context

In a noted recent article, Peter Steinberger has offered a very provocative critique of Quentin Skinner's methodology: namely, that the very philosophy upon which Skinner grounds his historical interpretation of texts — the 'philosophical pragmatics' as Steinberger calls it — are ill suited to the interpretation of written texts. The defining feature of this approach, according to Steinberger, is that it is used primarily to interpret improvised conversation and that improvised conversation requires a particular set of rules and conventions in order for it to be intelligible, whereas written communication does not require such rules. He does concede to the Skinnerian response that 'the author of a written text (. . .) is dependent upon and constrained by established discursive rules, just as much as the casual utterer'.[1] But this response, in Steinberger's mind,

Paragraph 34.3 (2011): 371–387
DOI: 10.3366/para.2011.0031
© Edinburgh University Press
www.eupjournals.com/para

is not sufficient because he believes 'that the particular kinds of rules that govern ordinary, improvised conversational activity and that are necessary for such activity to occur successfully must be quite different from the rules that govern formal writing' (*AHPT*, 139). Furthermore he insists that 'the burden of proof is on Skinner to show why this is not so' (*AHPT*, 139).

In this article I wish to take Steinberger up on his invitation, and in so doing I am prepared to accept that the burden of proof is upon me to demonstrate that the rules that govern ordinary improvised conversation are not significantly different from the rules that govern written communication. This question of the role that rules play in communication and the interpretation of communication is an important one, and in replying to Steinberger it is my hope to also point out that some fundamental issues are at stake in the practice of political philosophy. If I understand Steinberger correctly, in refuting the applicability of speech-act theory to textual interpretation he hopes to put the activity of political theory (or at the least that branch of political theory interested in the interpretation of historical texts of political theory) on a more 'analytical' footing — whereby interpretation would aim 'to reconstruct — patiently, systematically, and with close attention to the rules of rational inference — the argumentative structure of the text and its theoretical implications or entailments' (*AHPT*, 145).

In defending Skinner's method and the applicability of its philosophical underpinnings to political theory, I do not want to make all interpreters of historical texts Cambridge School theorists. Instead, I see Skinner as having been the first to introduce an approach to political philosophy that focused on action, use and meaning and that this approach has been far too neglected, and if I am correct then not only is Skinner's method valid, but the philosophical underpinnings of his method provide a sounder basis for doing political theory in general than the analytic method to which Steinberger would have us return. And so my hope is that this essay will clarify how the philosophy of Austin and Wittgenstein informs Skinner's approach to textual interpretation, and why the linguistic turn in philosophy matters for the historical study of political theory.

At the outset, it is worth noting that Steinberger does not attempt to refute any of the central claims of speech-act theory — that the meaning of an utterance is determined by its use in a particular context, that the successful performance of an utterance rests upon the satisfaction of a set of rules, and that failure to perform an utterance according to these rules will lead to misunderstanding and/or failing to do what one set out to do in performing a particular speech–act. Steinberger's objection is that speech–act theory does not apply to the interpretation of written texts. The challenge here is not to defend the method or orientation in general, it is to defend the application of this method in cases to which Steinberger thinks the method was not intended to — or simply cannot — apply. In Steinberger's understanding the approach pioneered by speech act theorists was to apply to improvised conversation, not to written texts.

Steinberger's assertion that ordinary language philosophy does not apply to written communication results from three errors in his reading of the connection between speech–act theory and Skinner's method. First, he has overemphasized the influence of Grice and Searle on Skinner's method and ignored entirely the influence of the later Wittgenstein.[2] This is significant because there are crucial differences between what Grice and Searle feel speech–act theory should do and what Austin and Wittgenstein themselves did. In overemphasizing the former and underemphasizing the later Steinberger has built up a straw man. Second, Steinberger insists that these philosophies of 'pragmatics of communication' 'are designed precisely to explain how the making and receiving of utterances functions successfully as an unrehearsed, improvised endeavour governed by communicative rules' (*AHPT*, 138). I will turn to the writings of J. L. Austin to show that his philosophy of language was not *only* (or even primarily) concerned with explicating improvised communication. As such, Skinner's appropriation of Austin shows us the value of treating texts as a performance rather than simply as a set of formal arguments. Third, I will argue that Steinberger draws a distinction between literal meaning and intended meaning that cannot be sustained. In conclusion, drawing upon remark §81 from Wittgenstein's *Philosophical Investigations*, I will argue that underlying Steinberger's understanding of how texts should be interpreted is a concept of an ideal language that Wittgenstein critiques. The reason Skinner's appropriation of philosophical pragmatics is useful is because he shows us how, given the insights of the linguistic turn, we can interpret historical texts.

The influence of philosophical pragmatics on Quentin Skinner's methodology

Steinberger's central critique of Skinner is that Skinner does not properly follow the implications of the theorists that he cites as the influence for his method (*AHPT*, 135). Steinberger has misread the role that these thinkers have played in Skinner's thought. Steinberger cites Austin, Searle and Grice as the chief influences upon Skinner's method, but in precisely the inverse proportion of their influence upon Skinner. Steinberger cites Grice seventeen times, whereas in *Regarding Method* — Skinner's collection of his methodological essays — he cites Grice four times.[3] Steinberger cites Austin sixteen times, whereas Skinner cites him twenty-four times. And Steinberger cites Searle sixteen times whereas Skinner cites him three times. Most strikingly, Steinberger cites Wittgenstein only once, and this reference is to the *Tractatus Logico-Philosophicus*, whereas Skinner cites the later Wittgenstein fifteen times and has said in a recent interview that: 'Insofar as I was able to understand the [*Philosophical Investigations*] at all, I took it to be about the theory of meaning, and I carried away from it a basic thought about "meaning" that subsequently animated all the essays I later published on that theme'.[4] As he makes clear in this interview, the philosophy of language of the later Wittgenstein is the primary philosophical inspiration for his methodology and his incorporation of Austin and Grice into his work are simply as 'annexes' to the ideas of Wittgenstein (*EP*, 48).

While counting the number of references in two different texts does not prove anything by itself, it is significant because Steinberger has drawn heavily upon Grice and Searle to reconstruct a model of 'philosophical pragmatics' that he then uses to accuse Skinner of failing to understand, suggesting that Skinner has failed to live up to a model of language that Skinner himself does not accept. The straw-man argument arises when Steinberger elides Austin with Searle and Grice, while remaining silent on the influence of the later Wittgenstein. Searle developed Austin's theory of performative utterances by exploring the constitutive rules for the successful performance of an illocutionary act, and Grice developed a theory of conversational implicature that explains the unstated, but implied meaning of a speech-act. In the cases of Searle and Austin, their primary interest is in human conversation, and their focus is on the rules that govern the improvisational structure of conversation. However, the work of Wittgenstein and Austin — unlike the work of Searle and Grice — is concerned with the performative nature of language in general *regardless of whether it is written or spoken*. As such, drawing upon Wittgenstein and Austin to analyse texts is completely consistent with their philosophy.[5] *Contra* Steinberger, philosophical pragmatics was intended to analyse more than just improvised conversation. But in arguing that it can only analyse speech–acts Steinberger introduces a second confusion: that of eliding improvisation with performativity as the object of analysis of philosophical pragmatics.

Improvisation vs performance and the role of rules

Another confusion that Steinberger exhibits concerning the nature of ordinary language philosophy is about what it is attempting to capture. Steinberger claims 'the speech–act theory of Austin and Searle and the implicative theory of Grice are designed to explain how the making and receiving of utterances functions successfully as an unrehearsed endeavour governed by competitive rules' (*AHPT*, 138). This is a point that he raises at several junctures to argue that the chief difference between the speech–acts that Austin, Searle and Grice analyse and the texts that Skinner examines is that speech–acts are improvised and texts are carefully written.

This claim is faulty for two reasons. First, Steinberger has confused performance with improvisation, as we have already noted. Second, the statement cuts against his claim that a recovering of intended meaning is not an important part of textual exegesis. In this case, Steinberger has misread the intention of Austin and Wittgenstein, who both argue that the meaning of an utterance is determined by how a statement is used in a particular context. Both Austin and Wittgenstein refute the notion that the meanings of words can be determined by knowing what material objects those words refer to — what philosophers of language call a referential theory of meaning. For both Austin and Wittgenstein the meaning of words is determined by their use in a particular context, regardless of whether or not a statement is rehearsed or improvised, spoken or written.

Yet speech-act theory was not intended only to recover the rules of improvised conversation. As Austin notes at the beginning of *How to Do Things with Words*, the purpose of his work was to look at statements that did not fit into the traditional categories of statements that analytic philosophers studied. Austin then proceeds to provide four such examples of statements: saying 'I do' at a wedding, naming a ship 'Queen Elizabeth' while smashing a bottle against its bow, saying 'I give and bequeath my watch to my brother,' and saying 'I bet you sixpence it will rain tomorrow'.[6] Now, Austin's point is that analytical philosophy has primarily focused upon what he calls 'constative' statements — that is statements that are true or false assertions of fact.

Conversely, Austin in *How to Do Things with Words* is developing a procedure for analysing performative statements — that is statements through which one performs an action.

Steinberger insists that the crucial feature of philosophical pragmatics is that it recovers rules that help make improvised speech possible (*AHPT*, 139). And as his evidence, he claims that most of the examples used by Austin, Grice and Searle are improvised speech acts (*AHPT*, 138). But in the case of the examples that Austin provides, most are rehearsed, not improvised. Weddings have rehearsals for a good reason: to make sure all the people in the party know when to say their lines. The 'I do' of a wedding is not off the cuff; the partners in the wedding are following a script. Similarly, an event like a christening of a ship is planned in advance, and all the people participating in the ceremony know their lines before the event. And a will, is 'a carefully planned, painstakingly executed, utterly non-improvised activity of asserting the actual or possible fact of a proposed content' to quote Steinberger's description of what a text is and a speech-act is not (*AHPT*, 141). Only the final case of a person making a bet could be considered an example of a spontaneous activity. Yet, even in the case of betting, one often (though not always) carefully analyses the situation and the likely outcome before calling one's bookie.

The crucial point here is that Steinberger insists that the philosophical pragmatics of Austin, Grice and Searle are not a good fit for interpreting texts in the history of political thought because their approach helps analyse improvised conversation. Yet this is not what Austin (who, of this trio, has the most influence on Skinner) is doing. Instead he focused on the performative dimension of language, be it written or spoken. Skinner adopted Austin's focus on the performative dimension of language for his methodology because he was concerned that the dominant approach to the history of political philosophy in the 1960s focused too much on looking in texts for perennial ideas. Instead, Skinner drew upon Austin and Wittgenstein because he felt that their approach to understanding the meaning of a statement by understanding the context in which that statement was used could help the intellectual historian 'consider what earlier philosophers may have been *doing* in writing as they wrote' (*RM*, 3). The point of Skinner's method is to understand how historic texts of political philosophy were written as interventions in particular political struggles.[7]

At the root of Steinberger's confusion is the role that rules play in language. Steinberger argues, 'that the particular kinds of rules that govern ordinary, improvised conversational activity and that are necessary for such activity to occur successfully must be quite different from the rules that govern formal writing' (*AHPT*, 139). In making this claim, Steinberger seems to ignore the large number of ways in which even written communication is not improvised but nevertheless follows many of the same rules as spoken conversation.[8] While written communication is revised and thought through in a way that a spontaneous conversation with a neighbour is not, as long as the communication is in the same language it draws upon the same set of rules as spoken communication. Many of these rules lie in the background, and are very difficult to explicate. If we had to be aware of all the rules of grammar and spelling and think through every possible way a word could be used or misinterpreted and think consciously about the muscle movement required to type or write even a single word we would go nowhere. We become conscious of the rules that govern our language when we slip up, when a sentence does not sound right. Writing follows these rules in the same way that improvised conversation does. Without these rules sitting in the background I would be unable to act, but if all the rules according to which I act were made explicit I would also be unable to act — paralyzed by my over analysis of how I should act.

All of this is to show that when we act in any way we are following rules. Steinberger's error is not simply in misunderstanding the scope of rules — that rules do not simply govern improvised speech — but more broadly in what rules do. Skinner's claim that to understand the meaning of an author's statement one must first explicate the linguistic conventions of the milieu in which the author wrote draws heavily on Wittgenstein's discussion of following rules in the *Philosophical Investigations*. The reason that Skinner draws upon Wittgenstein and Austin is because their philosophy of language points to a fundamental problem of textual interpretation: 'The problem of interpretation arises in part because we do not generally trouble, even in everyday cases, to make explicit exactly what we see ourselves as doing' (*RM*, 107). In reconstructing the discursive context in which a historical figure in political philosophy was writing Skinner is attempting to recover the rules that the figure was following. And in recovering the rules the figure was following, Skinner is attempting to understand what it is that figure was doing. Without an understanding of the background rules according to which authors were writing, their actions would be as unintelligible as trying to watch a sporting competition without understanding the rules of that game.[9]

It seems that Steinberger's confusion about how rules and conventions operate in language stems from his reliance on an analogy with jazz. To be fair, Steinberger's analogy is an illuminating one. Jazz, like language, is generally an improvised activity, and in order for a jazz piece to be successful — in the sense of pleasurable to listen to rather than random sound — the musicians must follow certain rules. In the *Philosophical Investigations* Wittgenstein introduces the concept of language games to describe 'language and the actions into which it is woven' (*PI*, §7). This concept is meant to illustrate that the meaning of a language is embedded in its use, and it is only through understanding how a word is used in a specific context that one can understand its meaning. Throughout the first eighty remarks in the *Philosophical Investigations* Wittgenstein proceeds to use the analogy between language and games to illustrate how we use language according to definite rules, and how an understanding of these rules is necessary in order to understand the meaning of words and concepts. Yet after developing this analogy Wittgenstein cautions against misunderstanding following a rule as 'operating a calculus according to definite rules' (*PI*, §81). This danger arises because games and calculi have 'fixed rules' (*PI*, §81). In drawing an analogy between the fixed rules of games and the rules that guide the uses of terms in a language the danger is to assume that these two types of rules operate in the same way. One can write out explicit rules about natural phenomena and rules of games, but to do this in a language would be to construct an ideal language. Yet such an ideal language would be a construction that would miss much of the nuance of everyday language. And Wittgenstein believes that to take the ideal language as somehow superior to our everyday language is what leads to confusions over the meanings of words and concepts. Steinberger seems to think that there are particular sets of rules that govern improvisation, and that philosophical pragmatics is concerned only with recovering those rules. Yet, the point of Wittgenstein's analysis of rules in language, and the reason that Skinner draws upon this aspect of Wittgenstein, is that discursive rules are not fixed. Some rules apply to both spoken and written conversation, other rules do not. And the nature of rules is challenged and modified over time. As such, the background rules according to which both speakers and writers make statements are constantly changing. And in order to understand the meanings of statements we must recover the rules according to which the statements were made.

The difficulty of separating the literal from the intended meaning in political philosophy

One of Steinberger's reasons for arguing that the philosophy of pragmatics is not applicable to the interpretation of texts of political philosophy is that there is a difference between the literal meaning and the intended meaning of a text. In order to illustrate this, Steinberger argues that we assert facts in order to refute scepticism about us engaging in a particular activity. Steinberger writes:

Thus, if I want simply to assert the fact of me calling your mother, and if I anticipate any scepticism, I may well be inclined to provide detailed evidence (e.g. a demonstration that I know how to reach your mother, proof that I have called your mother in similar circumstances), but, more important, I will often attempt to present my claim and my evidence in language — involving say, the use of force indicating devices — that minimizes or eliminates the difference between the literal meaning of my words and their intended meaning. (*AHPT*, 140)

Steinberger's point is that when political philosophers make propositional claims they will attempt to minimize the gap between the literal meaning of words and their intended meaning. So, one of the core points of Steinberger's critique of Skinner is that an attention to the illocutionary force of utterances focuses too much on the intended meaning of words as opposed to their literal meaning. Behind this critique is the assumption that there is some kind of gap between intended and literal meaning.

Steinberger thinks that understanding who and what an author was arguing against is irrelevant to understanding the propositional content of a political philosophy. This explains why he introduces a gap between assertions of fact and the intended meaning of a text. In doing this, Steinberger makes it sound as if political philosophy is a 'calculus operating according to definite rules' (to paraphrase Wittgenstein, *PI*, § 81). In order for this to be the case, all political philosophers would have to operate according to these definite rules in the construction of their arguments. Furthermore, this assumes that all political philosophers were attempting to make the arguments of their texts a series of transparent moves that abide by the rules of a single game that we would all recognize as political philosophy.

But consider for a second how different the type of enterprise that Plato engaged in is from Machiavelli's activities. Plato wrote dialogues, whereas Machiavelli wrote interpretations of historical figures in order to advise contemporary politicians. These differences in the genres shape the content of their arguments. In the case of Plato, while many assume that Socrates is often presenting Plato's perspective, a major area of debate within Plato scholarship is which characters in a dialogue (if any) speak for Plato. In the case of Machiavelli, his genre and style of writing have led to numerous questions about whether or not his suggestions were sincere.[10] So, at the very least the intended meaning of a text shapes our ability as readers to access the literal meaning of the text. And I would argue in the more 'literary' works — that is those works that deploy literary techniques such as metaphor, allegory, poetry, or narrative fiction in order to advance a normative argument about politics — in the political theory canon — such as the works of Plato, Machiavelli, Rousseau and Nietzsche — those authors chose to write in the style that they did because they did not feel that their message could be conveyed through 'literal' meanings.

While in many instances it may be difficult to separate the intended meaning from the literal meaning, Steinberger could reply that in successful works of political philosophy the author — intending to write a work that will stand the test of time — attempts to write a work that has as much literal content — assertions of fact and deductive arguments — and as little intended meaning — rhetorical content and literary style — as possible. And in many ways Hobbes's *Leviathan* is the best example of what Steinberger thinks political philosophy is. Recall that in *Leviathan*, Hobbes sets himself the task of discovering a new science of politics that is free from the erroneous assumptions of humanist political philosophy — a genre of political philosophy that placed a great deal of emphasis on the rhetorical skills of the authors. Instead, Hobbes wants to create a political philosophy that is simply a set of logical deductions from a set of empirical observations. In other words, Hobbes intended *Leviathan* to be a model of an approach to political philosophy that operates according to a set of rational rules that all can follow and reconstruct in their own mind. Yet, *Leviathan* is also marked by a scepticism that all will be able to understand the principles or that they will be willing to abide by them. So part of *Leviathan*'s argument is that the sovereign must force its subjects to follow these principles and definitions.[11] Hobbes goes to great lengths to define his terms precisely because he operates on the nominalist belief that words are mere signs that we affix to objects.

As Skinner demonstrates in *Reason and Rhetoric in the Philosophy of Hobbes*, while Hobbes was concerned about the destructive effect rhetoric could have in politics and the art of classical rhetoric was a target during the middle stage of Hobbes's career, by the time Hobbes writes *Leviathan* he has determined that rhetorical techniques are necessary to persuade an audience.[12] This is actually quite significant in the context of Steinberger's critique of Skinner, as Skinner's point in this book is that even that figure in the history of political philosophy most committed to developing a purely rational science of politics eventually had to conclude that rhetorical techniques are necessary to political argumentation. As such, Hobbes abandons the view of political philosophy as a context free civil science that operates according to literal meaning (in Steinberger's terms) in favour of one that acknowledges the role of rhetoric, and is sensitive to its audience and is involved in an act of persuasion rather than something akin to a scientific proof. In order for Steinberger's claim that interpreting texts in political philosophy is simply a matter of reconstructing the literal meaning of the arguments of the text to hold, he would have to demonstrate that the rhetorical form of the argument had no impact on the content of the argument. Yet, even someone as committed to a rational view of political argumentation as Hobbes, ultimately abandons this viewpoint. Furthermore, one of Skinner's points in recovering the classic art of political rhetoric in *Reason and Rhetoric* is to remind his readers that classic rhetorical techniques such as *paradiastole* are based on the principle that how a fact is described determines how others assess that fact in moral and political terms (*RR*, 91–5). In other words, classical rhetoricians realized that in the area of moral and political argumentation there was no such thing as a brute fact, all facts were interpreted through a moral outlook.

'Standing on the very brink of misunderstanding': the danger of presupposing an ideal language in political philosophy

Steinberger suggests as an alternative to contextual interpretation an analytic approach to philosophy. He argues that the purpose of an analytic approach to political philosophy is 'rationally reconstructing — perspicuously restating — what has been said in a way that reveals its underlying logic' (*AHPT*, 142). His view of textual analysis is to recast a philosopher in a better form. In critiquing Skinner he draws a distinction between a lexicographical analysis of a text — which involves reconstructing the grammatical rules of a particular discursive community — and a philosophical analysis that 'analyse[s] a particular set of propositions with a view towards discovering and explicating their underlying argumentative structure' (*AHPT*, 143). In making this distinction, Steinberger is arguing that Skinner is not involved in political philosophy, but that those who reconstruct the underlying logic or structure are. Furthermore, Steinberger proceeds to quote from Wittgenstein's *Tractatus:* 'Language disguises the thought, and indeed in such a way that from the external form of the clothes one cannot infer the form of the clothed thought'[13] and then asserts that 'this claim is every bit as relevant to his later work as it is to the *Tractatus* in which it appears' (*AHPT*, 143, n.13). This is a problematic claim, and from my perspective it is absolutely fatal to his argument against Skinner. Recall that the crux of Steinberger's critique is that the philosophical resources upon which Skinner draws 'actually point to a decidedly non-Skinnerian approach that focuses not primarily on discovering or reconstructing historical circumstances, but on uncovering and explicating structures of argumentation' (*AHPT*, 135). This is because the passage from the early Wittgenstein that Steinberger cites is precisely the claim that the later Wittgenstein rejects. And the reason for this rejection is that the later Wittgenstein comes to believe that the notion that there is an underlying logic behind all language and that the task of the philosopher is to recover this logic by clarifying language is wrong.

Wittgenstein explicitly rejects his earlier view of language in remark 81 when he writes:

[I]n philosophy we often *compare* the use of words with games and calculi which have fixed rules, but cannot say that someone who is using language *must* be playing such a game. — But if you say that our languages only *approximate* to such calculi you are standing on the very brink of misunderstanding. For then it may look as if what we were talking about were an *ideal* language. As if our logic were, so to speak, a logic for a vacuum. — Whereas logic does not treat of language — or of thought — in the sense in which a natural science treats of a natural phenomenon, and the most that can be said is that we *construct* ideal languages. But here the word 'ideal' is liable to mislead, for it sounds as if these languages were better, more perfect, than our everyday language; and as if it took the logician to show what a proper sentence looked like. (*PI, § 81*)

Wittgenstein adds that in his earlier work he made the mistake of thinking 'that if anyone utters a sentence and *means* or *understands* it he is operating a calculus according to definite rules' (*PI, § 81*). This error comes from the tendency to believe that there are a set of rules of logic that lie behind language, and that the task of the philosopher is to discover these rules. This drives philosophers to seek an abstract and universal mode of expression that is free from imprecision. But, as the later Wittgenstein argued, the rules of our language are embedded in our linguistic practices, and because our language is dynamic and changing, the meaning and use of words and the rules that govern how we use those rules change with our language. And this is precisely the reason that Skinner carefully reconstructs the discourses in which an author wrote: because their political language was different from ours. We will not understand their utterances without understanding the grammar of their political discourse. Conversely, Steinberger presupposes that there is a language beyond our everyday language that is universal in its structure regardless of which natural language an idea is expressed in and that this ideal language is unchanging across time and space. And because of this, the purpose of the analytic interpreter is to recast texts in this language.

There are three reasons why this claim is problematic. First, from the internal perspective of Steinberger's own argument — that is, that the philosophers of language that Skinner draws upon do not support Skinner's method — Steinberger has developed an argument that undercuts his own position. The type of analytic reconstruction of the logical arguments of a text that Steinberger holds up as the model of historical interpretation rests on precisely the view of language that Wittgenstein and Austin were rejecting. The later Wittgenstein's primary object of critique in the *Philosophical Investigations* was theories of ideal language. In its place, Wittgenstein argued that the meanings of words were determined by how words were used in specific contexts — that is language games — and that as such there was not one ideal meaning for a given word. Skinner draws upon this to argue that the meanings of words and utterances vary depending upon what historic and linguistic context a statement is used in. As such attempts to determine the transhistorical meaning of a text will fail because there is no ideal language or fixed meaning for words that the interpreter of a text can refer to in interpreting. Similarly, the element of J. L. Austin that Skinner draws upon is his argument that when one focuses on constative utterances (true/false statements), philosophers ignore a whole other class of statements, performative utterances (statements in which a person does something by uttering a series of words). Skinner takes from this the insight that works in political philosophy are not simply works of political *philosophy*, but that they are in fact primarily works of *political* philosophy. In other words, we will not understand a text if we simply focus on the truth content of that text's arguments, we must also understand what political acts the author was attempting to perform in writing that text. This type of understanding is only possible through an exploration of the author's political and historical context. As such, Skinner's method does follow from the philosophical resources that he draws upon. As discussed above, Wittgenstein and Austin are not simply developing a linguistic philosophy to deal with improvised conversation, their work was primarily interested in re-thinking what language is. In both cases they placed an emphasis on language as a practice or an activity — regardless of whether it was spoken or written — and they critiqued the idea that it was possible to construct an ideal language that could represent an objective world. The alternative model of textual interpretation the Steinberger suggests in his critique of Skinner rests on precisely such a picture theory of language. Yet Steinberger does not explain how he proposes to get around the critiques of this approach to language that Wittgenstein, Austin and other post-positivist analytic philosophers raised in the 1950s and 1960s. His approach is indeed very old-fashioned.

Second, there is a fundamental problem with presupposing that there is an ideal language that texts of political philosophy conceal. Why would political philosophers write in a language other than the one that Steinberger presupposes it is the task of the interpreter of historical texts to reconstruct those arguments in? While some political philosophers may have attempted to conceal their true intent[14] and others may simply be bad writers, if there were an ideal language in which to present arguments of political philosophy — say in symbolic logic — why wouldn't political philosophers have written their work in this manner in the first place? Steinberger seems to assume that political philosophy is like maths, and that political philosophers saw themselves (or at least they should see themselves) as constructing proofs that all readers would accept as true. Certainly there have been some political philosophers who have attempted to engage in such an activity. In some moments in *The Republic* Plato explores this possibility and Spinoza wrote his *Ethics* according to the geometric method. But if one surveys the canon of political philosophy, there have been as many different styles of writing political philosophy as there have been major political philosophers. This would suggest that Steinberger misunderstands what political philosophy is. It is not like maths, because arguments in political philosophy cannot be demonstrated in the way that a mathematical proof can be. Instead, arguments in political philosophy are attempts to persuade others. Persuasion presupposes that there are not self-evident truths as in mathematics, but that it is always possible to argue on either side of a given case, and that the rhetorical form of an argument shapes its content.

But even if we were to grant Steinberger that it was possible to re-construct arguments of texts in an ideal language, and that such a language would accurately reflect the argumentative content and intent of the writers of classic works of political philosophy, this raises another problem. Steinberger's description of what textual interpretation should be does not reflect how contemporary political theorists interpret texts in practice. Those who engage in the history of political thought have debates about the meaning and intention of works of political philosophy. Was Machiavelli a 'teacher of evil', a defender of republican virtues, or an ironist trying to trap Lorenzo de Medici?[15] Was Hobbes a proto-rational choice theorist, or was he using humanist rhetoric in order to critique humanist political values?[16] While Steinberger might dismiss such questions as merely 'lexographical', determining what an author's intentions are is essential to understanding the content of that author's argument (*AHPT*, 143). And while Steinberger assumes that most authors of political philosophy write works that are 'carefully written, rigorously argued, and painstakingly constructed assertions of proposed content' he does concede much scholarship in political theory provides evidence that authors write ironically, attempt to hide their message, and that sometimes their primary intent was to engage in a particularly provincial debate in their context. What he does not provide is a means to resolve these textual ambiguities. When two interpreters of Hobbes disagree over the meaning of Hobbes's text, what criteria should we use to adjudicate the dispute? The point of interpretive methods such as Skinner's is to provide us with such criteria. Yet the only method Steinberger provides us with is 'a systematic effort to focus closely on what is said, to piece together the structure of argumentation and to relate assertions of content with ever more accuracy and clarity' (*AHPT*, 143). While every good interpretation of a text should do this, what Steinberger does not explain is how one is supposed to do this in those instances where the structure of argumentation is ambiguous or the meaning of what is said is unclear. Finally, one might ask Steinberger what the point of the historical interpretation of political philosophy would be if it simply involved reconstructing the arguments of authors in a clear and logical form. If there is *a* clear and logical way in which to reproduce Hobbes's argument about the social contract, then once one scholar has written and published that reconstruction, why would we need any other works on Hobbes's social contract? In dismissing Skinner's method, Steinberger does not provide us with any guidance as to what would be a more appropriate means to interpret and analyse historical texts.

NOTES

1   Peter J. Steinberger, 'Analysis and History of Political Thought', *American Political Science Review* 103:1 (2009), 135–46 (139), henceforward *AHPT*.
2   The primary texts of Grice and Searle that Skinner and Steinberger refer to are: Paul Grice, *Studies in the Way of Words* (Cambridge, MA: Harvard University Press, 1989), and John Searle, *Speech Acts: An Essay in the Philosophy of Language* (Cambridge: Cambridge University Press, 1969).
3   Quentin Skinner, *Visions of Politics: Vol. 1. Regarding Method* (Cambridge: Cambridge University Press, 2002), henceforward *RM*.
4   Petri Koikkalainen and Sami Syrjämäki, 'Encountering the Past: An Interview with Quentin Skinner', *Finnish Yearbook of Political Thought* 6 (2002), 32–63 (47), henceforward *EP*.
5   The other major thinker of the twentieth century to do this is Stanley Cavell, who draws on Wittgenstein and Austin to analyse written and spoken language in as diverse a set of areas as film, theatre, contemporary music, epistemology and ethics. For example, see his diverse set of essays in Stanley Cavell, *Must We Mean What We Say? A Book of Essays* (Cambridge: Cambridge University Press, 1969, second edition 2002).
6   J.L.Austin, *How to Do Things with Words* (Cambridge, MA: Harvard University Press, 1962), 5.
7   See James Tully, 'The Pen is a Mighty Sword: Quentin Skinner's Analysis of Politics', in *Meaning and Context: Quentin Skinner and his Critics*, edited by James Tully (Cambridge: Cambridge University Press, 1988), 7–25.
8   I am paraphrasing here from Ludwig Wittgenstein, *Philosophical Investigations*, translated by G.E.M. Anscombe, 3rd edition (Oxford: Oxford University Press, 2001), §§199, 202, 211, 217, 219, henceforward *PI*. In this part of the *Philosophical Investigations*, Wittgenstein looks at the ways in which we follow rules in using language. These rules are constituted by the background of our social practices. For a more detailed analysis of this aspect of Wittgenstein and its implication for social and political philosophy see Charles Taylor, 'To Follow a Rule,' in *Philosophical Arguments* (Cambridge, MA: Harvard University Press, 1995), 165–80.
9   Compare with Wittgenstein, *PI*, §83.
10   For example see Mary Dietz, 'Trapping the Prince: Machiavelli and The Politics of Deception', *American Political Science Review* 80:3 (September

1986), 777–99. Dietz argues that Machiavelli is intentionally giving Lorenzo de Medici bad advice in order to return Florence to a republic.

11 Thomas Hobbes, *Leviathan* (Cambridge: Cambridge University Press, 1996), 31–2.

12 Quentin Skinner, *Reason and Rhetoric in the Philosophy of Hobbes* (Cambridge: Cambridge University Press, 1996), henceforward *RR*.

13 Ludwig Wittgenstein, *Tractatus Logico-Philosophicus* (London: Routledge and Keagan Paul, 1955), 4.002.

14 Compare Leo Strauss, *Persecution and the Art of Writing* (Glencoe: Free Press, 1952).

15 Compare the interpretations of Machiavelli's *The Prince* offered in Dietz, 'Trapping the Prince' to Leo Strauss, *Thoughts on Machiavelli* (Chicago: University of Chicago Press, 1995) and to Quentin Skinner, *Visions of Politics: Renaissance Virtues*, vol. 2 (Cambridge: Cambridge University Press, 2002).

16 Compare Skinner, *RR* to David Gauthier, *The Logic of Leviathan: The Moral and Political Theory of Thomas Hobbes* (Oxford: Clarendon Press, 1969).

Wittgenstein's *Philosophical Investigations*, Linguistic Meaning and Music

Garry L. Hagberg

Abstract:

This article undertakes a comparison between Wittgenstein's philosophy of the early and late periods with the musical theories of Wittgenstein's contemporary, Heinrich Schenker, an influential Viennese theorist of tonality, as well as those of their contemporary Arnold Schoenberg. Schenker's reductive analytical procedure was designed to unveil fundamental and uniform ways in which all works of music function (and *should* function), unfolding a deep structure constituting their essence. Schoenberg deplored this line of thought, and for reasons strikingly parallel to those that led Wittgenstein back to what he called the 'rough ground' in his *Philosophical Investigations*. Ultimately, for Wittgenstein, the abstracted picture of the musical work as a platonic entity is nourished by grammatical conflations as well as by the Platonic and Cartesian legacies.

Keywords: Wittgenstein, Heinrich Schenker, Schoenberg, music, tonality, analysis, essentialism

Because philosophy for Wittgenstein is an *activity*, specifically that of excavating the presumptions that lead to multiform conceptual confusions — where those confusions arise as a result of 'the bewitchment of our intelligence by means of language' — philosophy is not accurately describable as a process of moving from a stable philosophical problem to a stable or settled philosophical doctrine that answers that problem. This claim does not by any means suggest (as some have mistakenly believed) that thus for Wittgenstein or for work in the Wittgenstinian tradition philosophical progress is not possible — quite the contrary. But the nature or character of that progress will be very much unlike the progress–toward–doctrines of conventional

Paragraph 34.3 (2011): 388–405
DOI: 10.3366/para.2011.0032
© Edinburgh University Press
www.eupjournals.com/para

philosophy, or the kind of progress that is modelled on a simplified picture of science. We see in Wittgenstein's lectures on aesthetics that he has little patience for the scientific–deductive model applied to the thinking and processes of critical reasoning that lead to our evaluative judgements (for example: 'All good works of music have x; this work has x; ergo . . .'). That falsification, or psychological misconstrual of the character of aesthetic perception, reflection and judgement, not only fails to acknowledge the great significance of relational comparisons as they both give content to and refine aesthetic perception, but it also fails to preserve a space in aesthetic reflection for reasons of a kind that are not the direct result of (deductive) *reasoning*.[1] In short, any such deductive falsification leads us to do nothing less than to miscast severely the entire nature of our aesthetic engagements from the outset; one measure of the severity of such miscasting is the difficulty one then has in escaping the influence, explicit of otherwise, of the deductive model.

A methodological revolution

It is now easy to forget what a radical break Wittgenstein's mature work of *Philosophical Investigations* constituted: Frege saw both the philosophy of logic and the philosophy of mathematics as 'a science of abstract entities',[2] and Russell, for all his changing development over a life of thought, never for a moment doubted the deep continuities between science and philosophy. Indeed his harsh criticism of Wittgenstein's later work along just these lines — and his failure to comprehend both the content and spirit of that work — is recorded in his remark, 'The later Wittgenstein seems to have grown tired of serious thinking and to have invented a doctrine which would make such an activity unnecessary.'[3] And of course the tradition of methodological scientism, if in many guises, goes back through the history of philosophy to Plato: Platonism is a world of abstract entities to which philosophy gives access; Aristotelianism, while not that, is scientific-minded in its giving descriptions and explanations of the nature of reality (particularly in the *Metaphysics*); Cartesian philosophy deduces the way the world must be independent of its untrustworthy appearances; Empiricism purports to investigate the features of the world through the scrutiny of atomistic sense-perception; Romanticism describes the trans-empirical nature of reality; and much of twentieth-century philosophy before Wittgenstein, during Wittgenstein (particularly in positivism),[4] and after Wittgenstein (in Quine et al.),[5] is quite evidently in a scientific mould. Perhaps the most telling exception to the rule is Kant, and it is no accident that in the early interpretations of Wittgenstein's later philosophy the similarities to Kantian methodology were perhaps overemphasized.[6] Kant's concern, indeed his 'Copernican Revolution', was to give an account not of the external world, but of the conditions – or rather preconditions – of the possibility of experiencing that world. The reversal that constituted his Copernican revolution changed the focus from external reality to the mind's contribution in structuring our experience of that reality. Wittgenstein can hardly be called a Kantian, but there is, broadly speaking, a clearly discernible thematic affinity, and Wittgenstein's own methodological revolution in philosophy was one that, in 1930, he called a 'kink' in the history of thought that profoundly interrupted the status quo, of a kind, as he himself described it, 'comparable to the Galilean revolution in science'.[7] The analogy is in truth somewhat less than perfectly apt — Wittgenstein's was a revolution *against* the field-wide influence of the image of science in philosophy, but his description of his own revolution does convey a sense of the magnitude of his methodological intervention. That method[8] (or actually collection of methods, approaches, and techniques for changing the way we see a problem and the entire problem-field within which it is situated) made it possible to achieve a new and perspicuous view of our multiform human practices and what is manifest within them, through clusters of questions concerning language (for example: meaning, sense, context, coherence, intelligibility, limits of the expressible, philosophical grammar, the arbitrary and the non-arbitrary, misleading analogies, conceptual conflations, etc.) and clusters of questions concerning mind (for example: intention, will, memory, reading, expectation, expression, the inner, etc.). And in focusing on these problem-areas, in conceptually clarifying them, Wittgenstein gave an unprecedented degree of nuanced attention to language not as it is theorized in the abstract, not as it is envisaged as ideal in the philosophical imagination, but as it is *used* in the vast complex of practices collected under the term 'communication'. In *Philosophical Investigations* he wrote, 'Philosophy may in no way interfere with the actual use of language; it can in the end only describe it.'[9] And those descriptions, given at a level of detail regarded as unnecessary in previous philosophy (and again in much philosophy since), in breaking us free from false or oversimplified conceptual models, brought philosophical progress with them.

Much like the young author of the *Tractatus*, Frege, Russell and many other 'ideal-language' theorists[10] posited as a requirement of serious thinking (to which Russell referred above) the 'crystalline purity' of logic as it was thought to reside beneath the messier surface of language. But now, in *Philosophical Investigations*, Wittgenstein has effected a great change (indeed one of Galilean proportions) in his way of seeing the matter, just as he, as author, shows the routes to such a change for his readers. In §107 he wrote:

> The more narrowly we examine actual language, the sharper becomes the conflict between it and our requirement. (For the crystalline purity of logic was, of course, not a *result of investigation*: it was a requirement.) The conflict becomes intolerable; the requirement is now in danger of becoming empty. — We have got on to slippery ice where there is no friction and so in a certain sense the conditions are ideal, but also, just because of that, we are unable to walk. We want to walk: so we need *friction*. Back to the rough ground!

For him, now, the very possibility of serious thought is afforded by *escaping* the vision-narrowing and template-imposing influence of the scientific model, and not, as Russell maintained to the end, by sticking to it.[11]

This profound methodological change holds, I believe, considerable significance for our understanding of music, for our way of seeing our diverse musical practices. And one strikingly clear place to see this is in the debate that erupted between Arnold Schoenberg and the great Viennese musical theorist Heinrich Schenker.

Schoenberg and Schenker

Just as the Viennese positivists were concerned to reveal the means of verification for any proposition or utterance, where those means of verification would underwrite and guarantee the meaningfulness of the proposition, so Schenker was concerned to reveal the underlying base structure of a work of music, where that structure would both underwrite and guarantee the coherence or sense of the work. For those theorists of language, the buried structure, once revealed, could serve as the foundation over which the (for them) structurally-irrelevant differentia on the level of communication could be seen (and largely dismissed), just as for Schenker the *Urlinie*, the underlying compositional line or thread, could serve as the backdrop over and against which other mid-level and surface-level musical events could be seen (and accorded an irremediably secondary status). And like the linguistic theorists, Schenker's reductive analytical procedure was one believed capable of laying bare the fundamental and uniform way in which *all* works of music, in their underlying essence if not in their local details and decorative prolongations, function. Like the linguistic views, Schenker's system is not without complexity, but to simplify greatly, the leading idea of this grand theory of universal musical structure is that, resting beneath all the variety on the sonic surface, all the melodic and harmonic events that particularize the composition in question, the buried invariant harmonic structure of movement, over the long form of the piece, progresses from the tonic to the dominant, and — to reach the culmination of the work's organicist or internally-developing teleology — back again to the tonic. (Tonic and dominant chords, as the two most fundamental chords in a diatonic harmonic system, are built on the first and the fifth scale-steps respectively, where the tonic defines the key, and where the dominant, because of its internal tension, as we say 'wants' to resolve or return to the 'home' of the tonic.) For Schenker, this tonic-dominant-tonic progression (conventionally notated 'I-V-I') is an essential condition of all well-structured music (indeed all great music, and we should note that this thus functions for Schenker as a deductively-derivable criterion of quality: All great works have x; this work has x; ergo...).

At a glance one can see the monumental implausibility of such a view,[12] but to understand Schenker, one has to see that that is indeed just Schenker's point. *At a glance*, one sees a rather large number of surface-level harmonic movements and progressions that are, as any student of harmonic analysis knows, anything other than I-V-I. Schenker's theory stands — roughly speaking — parallel to the kind of deep structure analysed in Chomskian linguistics: the seemingly endless variation we see on the surface of linguistic praxis is in fact, under the dictates of the Cartesian system, *reduced*, through transformational processes, to what is construed as their underlying essence.[13] Schenker developed an intricate process of similar transformations, in such a way that surface-level variety is reduced to deep-structure uniformity: it is as though the ideal musical language, the 'crystalline purity' of music, rests hidden beneath the misleadingly diversified surface. This analysis was carried out in the image of science and worked through in search of, if not exactly abstract entities, then certainly abstract structures to which the depth-analysis provided access. The actual embodied *experience* of music is pushed to the periphery of relevance, as are the seemingly endless nuanced particularities of diverse compositions that, in truth, make the individual pieces what they are.[14] It is what they have *in common* (this recalls the platonic picture of class-membership), and what is available to the intellect (through score analysis) rather than the senses, that attracts Schenker's attention. That, he believes, is what constitutes the genuine content of serious musical thought. He is, in short, the theorist most perfectly tailored to the tradition against which Wittgenstein's methodological revolution is reacting, and — as is true of the parallel figures in philosophy — he is hardly a solitary figure in the history of musical analysis.

It is possible, and indeed interesting, to work out connections between the Wittgenstein of the *Tractatus Logico-Philosophicus* and Schoenberg's serial technique: both (1) describe underlying organizational structures that generate sense — here particularly the perceived sets of relations between parts within a sentence or a work that yield propositional or thematic coherence; both (2) demarcate the limits of (verbal or musical) intelligibility (that is, the ability of a perceiver or sentence or work to make sense of what is given to linguistic or aesthetic experience, to discern interconnectedness, and to quickly judge degrees of relevance ranging from the immediately germane to the disorientingly unrelated; and both (3) develop a vision of combinatorial possibility, thus providing a sense to the hearer of what can and cannot be done, what moves are and are not possible, within the verbal exchange or within the musical composition. But in the debate with Schenker, Schoenberg, it turns out, is, if initially somewhat surprisingly, more a fellow traveller of the *later* Wittgenstein.[15] Why, exactly?

The heart of Schoenberg's debate with Schenker concerned the determination of the definitional criteria for what does, and what does not, constitute a chord. The intuitively plausible definition, a stack of pitches sounding simultaneously, is objectionably over-simple for Schenker because it ignores the question of the *function* of such simultaneities within the unfolding of the underlying contrapuntal structure. This point — a larger one than it may initially seem — was central to his very strategy of reductionism: if many of the vertically-stacked sonorities in a composition could be deprived of chord identity, then they could be seen as mere passing vertical consequences of melodic movement through a number of instrumental (or, in vocal music, actual) voices, thus leaving a much reduced number of chords to account for — and to be forced into the mould of dominant-tonic relations — within the structural long-form of the piece. Moreover, if all vertical sonorities that are unstable in nature are excluded, i.e. all those vertical sonorities that assemble pitches *other* than those of traditional diatonic harmony, the I-V-I under-skeleton becomes not only more visible (by a process of designed harmonic attrition), but that structure will then seem to be, indeed, nothing less than the essence of the piece around which all the non-chordal sonorities revolve. All dissonant vertical combinations of pitches are for Schenker designated non-chords on grounds of the internal tension that produces a teleological drive toward resolution in the triad (a consonant, and thus for him, actual chord), just as grammatical nuances and differentiations were designated irrelevant to the posited underlying ideal structure of logical atomism.

Schoenberg deplored this entire line of musical-analytical thought, and for reasons strikingly parallel to those that led Wittgenstein back to the 'rough ground' in *Philosophical Investigations*. James K. Wright vividly describes the debate, and given the evidence he adduces it is clear that Schoenberg did not regard any dissonance as sufficient to disqualify a vertically stacked sonority of chordal identity. In fact, for Schoenberg, 'everything that sounds simultaneously'[16] is a chord, and the fact that such chords may be arrived at by linear contrapuntal (horizontal) movement is hardly sufficient grounds to deny them a vertical identity. And if they do then possess full chordal identity, they resist the Schenkerian reduction to an essential I-V-I substructure and deserve full analytic attention *as structural entities in their own right*. That analytical attention will reveal the distinct, context-specific, highly individual character of those chords *in situ*: it will reveal the *differences* that make them what they are, where those differences emerge through a comparative or indeed relational analysis of nuanced particularities. (Recall that Wittgenstein considered using King Lear's 'I'll show you differences!' as a motto for his later work.) Schoenberg sees in Schenker (to use Wittgenstein's very phrases from his *Blue Book*) a contemptuous attitude toward the particular case, a craving for generality, and perhaps a preoccupation with the methods of science, that together blind Schenker's analysis to the *differentia* that feed just the kind of particularized relational-aesthetic understanding about which Wittgenstein lectured in 1930–33 and 1938. (And those lectures are very much deepened when contextualized into the other work he did from the *Blue Book* forward in pursuit of telling, instructive, and conceptually liberating *differentia* in the study of language and mind.)

The specific phraseology of Schoenberg's defence of the particular case is itself suggestive of the debate that the later Wittgenstein had with the atomistic analytical program, i.e. a program wherein the working out of the system is fundamental, and then any particular specimen of linguistic usage will be of analytical interest only insofar as it illustrates that system in whole or part. Schoenberg wrote, 'I maintain that these are chords, not of the system, but of music. Somebody will object: 'Yes, but they just happen by virtue of the passing tones.' I shall reply: 'The seventh and the ninth chord likewise just happened by virtue of passing tones before they were accepted into the system'.'[17] In short, their *use* within music is *prior to*, and decidedly not (in practice or in theory) posterior to, the system into which we may place them; their systematic function (i.e. their identities as given by the analytical nomenclature of a superimposed system) is a function of mere nominalism, and not an analytical revelation of their invariant essence.[18] Schoenberg's emphasis on *sound* (and his attendant scorn for an over-emphasis on the score) is also, I would suggest, another manifestation of his fundamental insight into the primacy of use-in-context as the determinant of (musical) sense: he wrote, 'What else is the appoggiatura but an embarrassed concession that the ear with its sharp perception, makes to the slow-witted eye? Here something is supposed to sound whose notation the eye cannot tolerate . . . . One's inability to regard it as a chord does not mean it is not a chord, but rather that (if it does not resolve) it is not like any of those that appear in the system.'[19] Schenker, in a manner reminiscent of Russell, believed to the end that the discovery of the underlying logical (in his case musicological) form was primary, to which all other musical phenomena, heard and seen, were subordinate. And, also like Russell, he believed to the end that serious analytical work could only proceed in that mould. Schoenberg, in a manner reminiscent of the later Wittgenstein, came to see music — for Schoenberg, 'music' referred never to a static thing but rather to an ever-expanding network of the equivalents in music of language-games — as a vast landscape of incrementally-expanding, sense-generating compositional practices.[20]

It must be said here that one could argue that Schoenberg's own compositional practices actually support a good deal more of the Russellian-Schenkerian line of thought than I have indicated, precisely because Schoenberg's twelve-tone rows often seem to imply harmonic 'resting places', or, in short, they seem to repeatedly generate flashes of triad-based harmonic stability (if of a fleeting kind). That would suggest that the underlying logic of harmony is (as it is believed always to be, for Schenker) nevertheless functioning, despite the official renunciation of it in the stated theory of serial composition. In short, the underlying logic would then show itself (as an incontrovertible triumph for Schenker) to be sufficiently strong to bring even those practices explicitly designed to refute it into alignment with it. But Glenn Gould captures the reality of the compositional situation here well, showing that this is not the case, and Gould's remarks implicitly point to yet another linkage between Schoenberg's actual practices and the thought of the later Wittgenstein, as that thought stands as a Galilean alternative to Russellian and Schenkerian structural metaphysics. Gould writes:

To be sure, the line dividing tonality from the appearance of tonally reminiscent sequences is not always easy to define in Schoenberg's later works, because the arbitrary selection of motivic material upon which he settled as sponsor of his twelve-tone structures tends with the later works to become more dependent upon interval connections which, if not in themselves tonally reminiscent, are at least triadically reminiscent. Schoenberg's fondness for the sort of row that would provide him with a series of triad forms was prompted less by an interest in triads per se than by a concern for finding twelve-tone situations in which the two halves of the row would not only be complementary in terms of their division of the chromatic scale but would also emphasize similar interval combinations within both antecedent and consequent portions. The reasons for this concern with interval duplication can be summarized as a desire to achieve total chromatic equilibrium while concentrating upon stringently controlled motivic resources: in effect, the principle of diversity within unity that governs practically all of Schoenberg's works is here expressed in terms peculiar to twelve-tone organization.[21]

One thus hears triadically reminiscent passages, but those moments, rightly understood, are generated *internally* within the serial row (and not from beneath it in a deep structure of universal musical grammar) as a consequence of Schoenberg's desire to find and preserve the compositional equilibrium between the first and second halves of the twelve-tone row. The musical grammar functioning here is one in which Schoenberg puts into play a demarcated set of combinatorial possibilities as a result of the ordering of the chromatic scale within the row in just the way Gould has described; in short, it is the direct musical analogue to a later-Wittgenstinian language-game. And the new linkage to which Gould's remarks point is this: grammatical coherence, for the later Wittgenstein, is *internal* to our linguistic practices, and not the surface-level result of a hidden or submerged world of Russellian logical clarity. The neo-Hutchesonian principle of diversity-within-unity to which Gould refers is thus a principle of Schoenberg's composition, but a principle that one sees worked out, applied, extended, altered, bent, mutated and so forth *within* his compositional practices. It is not a principle, as a compositional equivalent of an invariant and submerged grammatical rule, that precedes – and thus both dictates and circumscribes – the practices. It is rather, and in a way deeply consistent with the later Wittgenstein's work on philosophical grammar, a *working* principle; it is not the musical analogue to the invariant way in which an arithmetic rule determines a numerical series.[22]

Fairly early in the self-interrogative unearthing of the hidden presuppositions, conceptual pictures, and intellectual temptations that lead us into polarized theories, false dichotomies, and over-generalizations in *Philosophical Investigations*, Wittgenstein is discussing the idea — an idea possessing a long, distinguished, historically entrenched, and deeply misleading legacy of philosophical and linguistic work leading up to it — that language is, in essence, a set of assertions, and that linguistic usage just is, in essence, the making of these. Against this massively oversimplifying and blinding presumption, Wittgenstein asks (in *PI*, §23): 'But how many kinds of sentences are there? Say assertion, question, and command? — There are *countless* kinds: countless different kinds of use of what we call 'symbols', 'words', 'sentences'. And this multiplicity is not something fixed, given once for all; but new types of language, new language-games, as we may say, come into existence, and others become obsolete and get forgotten.'[23] One can well imagine Schoenberg answering the question, 'How many kinds of musical themes are there?' in much the same way. If one were to give the answer, 'Three — there are the 'assertions' of thematic statement, the 'questions' of the antecedents in antecedent-consequent (or indeed 'question-answer') phrase structure, and the 'commands', the powerful major themes in marches and military music, Schoenberg might well say (and readings of his *Theory of Harmony* and *Style and Idea*[24] encourage just such an extrapolation), 'There are countless kinds.' And the breaking of the hold of the notion, the picture, of reducible uniformity might well be accomplished in just the same way as in Wittgenstein's intellectual project: he adds (in *PI*, §23), 'Here the term 'language-games' is meant to bring into prominence the fact that the *speaking* of language is part of an activity, or of a form of life.' Without exception the use occurs *in context*, and it is there and only there that the point, the purpose, the tone, the gesture, the hint, the innuendo, the insinuation, the overture, the indirection, the bluntness, the humour, the spirit, the letter, the implication, or a thousand other things possess relationally embedded sense. Schoenberg saw the corresponding deep truth about music, and it is clear, given his remarks on music when taken within their larger philosophical context, Wittgenstein did as well. There are, for Wittgenstein, 'countless different kinds of use of what we call "symbols", "words", "sentences"' (*PI*. §92), and there are — as Schoenberg enunciated the point in opposition to Schenker's superimposed uniform template — countless different kinds of use of contextually seated and idiomatically differentiated chords, harmonies, dissonances, resolutions, themes, statements, subjects, motifs, and so forth. And these uses are no more fixed in advance of our multiform practices in music then they are in language — they are not, in Wittgenstein's words, 'given once for all'.

There is a more-than-gentle irony in the fact that the very composer in Wittgenstein's own time who brought 'a new type of language, a new language-game' into our expanding web of musical praxis, moreover one arguing against the subordination of the telling particular to overarching theory, was one in whom Wittgenstein – owing to a conservative musical sensibility conjoined to a Spenglerian conception of cultural decline that for him began just after Brahms – had utterly no interest. Schoenberg's language (in his theoretical writings), and his musical language (in his compositions, particularly those after *Verklärte Nacht* when the serial 'language-game' was gradually consolidated and stylistically solidified) move, along lines deeply analogous to those laid down by the Wittgenstein of the *Blue and Brown Books* and, as we have glimpsed here, *Philosophical Investigations*. Each found the friction required for forward movement on the rough ground.

Two separability theses

There is another dimension of Wittgenstein's thought in the period of *Philosophical Investigations* that is also centrally relevant to our gaining a deeper understanding of how he saw music as a profoundly meaningful art form (in a manner free of misleading models of meaning). Wittgenstein writes, in *PI* §24, 'If you do not keep the multiplicity of language-games in view you will perhaps be inclined to ask questions like: "What is a question?"' Given an intellectual genealogy that traces back through Cartesianism to Platonism, we have seen many in the history of modern musical aesthetics ask 'What is — or what *kind* of thing is — a musical work?' The platonistic influence yields, as we saw above, a fundamental concern with musical ontology, where the musical work is thought to be a distinct kind of abstract entity separate from, and prior to, the rich and multifarious (and indeterminately bounded, but that is another issue) collection of human actions and engagements involving that work. (Set theory, in platonic garb, can fairly easily be discerned in the undercurrents here, shaping what we see on the surface as the musical version of the ancient problem of the one and the many.) And the Cartesian element would then add to the mix by separating what we would call the meaning of the work from the materials of music within which we will then see that meaning as embodied, or as a physicalized form of its mental predecessor or imaginary prototype. Thus the Platonic-Cartesian combined legacies have produced two conjoined separability theses: (1) that the musical work is separable from and logically prior to its instantiations, and (2) that the meaning of that work is separable from and prior to its embodiment in its sound (emphasizing matter) or score (emphasizing mind).

Wittgenstein's later work on language (and on mathematics, although that too is a separate story) undercuts both of these separability theses in connection with the traditional problems of word-meaning and sentence-meaning, and it does so without reducing the linguistic phenomena in question to any version (explicit or otherwise) of behaviouristic[25] monism. Such separations, such bifurcations, are part and parcel of the over-generalized theory that desensitizes thought to significant particularity or that diminishes our capacity for a sustained attention to particulars. The actual work of Wittgenstein's later phase, undertaken over many years and throughout many notebooks, typescripts, and drafts, is impossible to summarize (and instructively so), but for present purposes it may be helpful to ask why, for all his conceptual acuity and his profound attachment to music and musical experience, did Wittgenstein never in his remarks on music take up, even in passing, the problem of musical ontology, and why did he never address the question asking about *the* nature of *the* relation between music and meaning? The answer, I would suggest, is that his extensive work on the philosophy of language that undercut these twin separability theses inoculated him against the posing of the parallel questions in musical form. His writings on music show, not at all merely an ignoring of these twin questions, one platonic and one Cartesian, but rather an earned freedom from them. Wittgenstein's way of speaking about music itself resists falling back into the traditional grooves (recall his opening sentence in his lectures on aesthetics — specifically that the entire subject is misunderstood),[26] and taken together his remarks on music intimate a way of seeing the art-form that is conceptually liberated from these inherited dichotomies. But, in understanding this point, it is essential to bear in mind that Wittgenstein does not have a *theory* of language that summarily precludes or neatly refutes such separation-theses; rather, he encourages, over an expansive terrain of philosophical reflection, a changed way of seeing wherein it is the actual *practices* of our multiform linguistic engagements are seen genuinely to make sense, and by a contrast that then becomes available, the over-generalized questions of theory-driven philosophers concerning the meaning of a word (as we can come to see through sufficiently attending to particulars — of just the kind Schoenberg defended against Schenker) do not.[27] At both early and later points in *Philosophical Investigations*, Wittgenstein appeals to our natural history in connection with questions of language; language is not the embodiment of a prior and separable ideal system, nor it is the materialization of Cartesian pre-linguistic inner content only contingently externalized. It is, as he says in §25, an inextricably interwoven part of our natural history: 'Commanding, questioning, recounting, chatting, are as much a part of our natural history as walking, eating, drinking, playing'. This remark is offered as a corrective against the impulse to (what he called) 'sublime' the logic of our language, to remove it from *this* world, or — as philosophers of language have long been prone to do — speak of language as though we are disembodied. And much later in the book, in §415, looking back over his own work, he writes, 'What we are supplying are really remarks on the natural history of human beings; we are not contributing curiosities however, but observations which no one has doubted, but which have escaped remark only because they are always before our eyes.'

Wittgenstein knew that music, like language, is an inseparable and irreducible part of our form of life, and although he said at one point that only aesthetic questions really gripped him — *these* separability-thesis questions within the philosophy of art and music never gripped him, because they are in truth merely the aesthetic variants of generalized linguistic questions the intelligibility of which he had already, as a result of sustained labours, very much called into question. They are questions that do not, and will not — indeed because they cannot — yield the distinctive kind of insight that is constitutive of aesthetic understanding. Musical theorists and aestheticians have all too easily spoken of music as though the embodied nature of music making in all its variations is only a contingency, as though musical works are platonic abstractions, as though musical meaning originates within a hermetically sealed Cartesian interior. By the time Wittgenstein wrote his post-*Tractatus* remarks on music, he was immune to this particular way of attempting to sublime the logic of music: he sees that it is part of our natural history, and his remarks on it collectively reveal this conceptual orientation. The identity of a musical work is not separable from our myriad practices, any more than the act of meaning something is separable from the real and live human conditions of speech. One does not mean something as a hermetically sealed imaginative act, nor does one will something, or intend something, without the complex of circumstances within which one means, wills, or intends. Conceptual *pictures* of meaning, of willing, of intending would divorce the actions from their contexts, from indeed the preconditions of their intelligible uses, but those pictures — as we have seen in Wittgenstein's *Philosophical Investigations* and in work going back to the time of the *Blue Book* and to his lectures on aesthetics — falsify and obscure far more than they accurately describe (where accurate and detailed description, as we saw above, can be and very often is the instrument of philosophical progress).

Meaning something in music, like intending something musically or willing something musically, takes place within the experiential preconditions of their possibility (to again sound the Kantian theme). One does not mean or intend or will solely in one's hermetic imagination; nor does a composer compose solely therein, nor does a conductor solely conduct therein. In a foot-of-page note in *Philosophical Investigations* (18), Wittgenstein asks, 'Can I say "bububu" and mean "If it doesn't rain I shall go for a walk"?', and he answers — against the impulse to platonize, to sublime, to picture the mental as wholly contained within itself, '– It is only in a language that I can mean something by something. This shows clearly that the grammar of "to mean" is not like that of the expression "to imagine" and the like.' Composers, conductors, performers, and listeners do indeed engage their musical imaginations in countless ways, but those multiform imaginative acts take place *within*, and not prior to, the stream of musical life that makes them possible. Nor is that extensive musical life reducible to an essence of *an* act of musical imagination, a paradigm mental act that constitutes the pre-embodied core of music and musical meaning around which all musical actions revolve and upon which they are dependent — and to which (to make the music-language analogy at work here explicit) we would then think they refer in order to fix their determinate content. The grammars of all these myriad actions are not reducible to a uniform grammar of imagining.[28] The abstracted picture of the musical work as a platonic entity behind or above what we will then call its 'manifestations', or the 'type' behind what we will then think of as its 'tokens', is nourished by just such grammatical conflations as well as by the Platonic and Cartesian legacies. Wittgenstein's remarks on music, like his far more extensive remarks on language and mind, show a sustained and heightened sensitivity to just such differences (differences that, like Lear, he has indeed shown), and taken together they point us to a way of speaking about music that evinces a humane mindfulness of the preconditions, and the lived, embodied realities, of musical intelligibility.

NOTES

1   On this point see M.W. Rowe, 'Criticism without Theory', in *Philosophy and Literature: A Book of Essays* (Aldershot: Ashgate, 2004), 22–45.

2   I borrow this phrase from Hans-Johann Glock's helpful discussion of Wittgenstein on philosophical method in *A Wittgenstein Dictionary* (Oxford: Blackwell, 1996), 293.

3   This is insightfully discussed in Ray Monk, *How to Read Wittgenstein* (New York: W.W. Norton, 2005), 68.

4   On this point see James K. Wright, *Schoenberg, Wittgenstein, and the Vienna Circle* (New York: Peter Lang, 2004).

5   The contrast is most lucidly and exactingly made (and where the central concept of fact, as it operates centrally in Quine's philosophy, is enlighteningly shown to usher in an ultimately unintelligible form of scepticism which has no point of entry in Wittgenstein's philosophy), in Jane Heal, *Fact and Meaning: Quine and Wittgenstein on Philosophy of Language* (Oxford: Blackwell, 1989).

6   On this matter see the instructive comparison between the first and second editions of P.M.S. Hacker's *Insight and Illusion* (Oxford: Oxford University Press, 1972), where the subtitle of the first edition is 'Wittgenstein on Philosophy and the Metaphysics of Experience' and the second is 'Themes in Wittgenstein's Philosophy'; a comparison of the two editions, and the way Hacker recast the second edition, makes the point nicely and powerfully shows how important can be a difference of emphasis and the situating of a text historically.

7   See Glock, *A Wittgenstein Dictionary*, 292.

8   I pursue this point at greater length in *Describing Ourselves: Wittgenstein and Autobiographical Consciousness* (Oxford: Clarendon Press, 2008), in the section

'On Philosophy as Therapy: Wittgenstein, Cavell, and Autobiographical Writing', 240–57.

9   Ludwig Wittgenstein, *Philosophical Investigations*, translated by G.E.M. Anscombe, 3rd edition (Oxford: Oxford University Press, 2001), §124. Henceforward *PI*.

10   For arguments for and against the ideal-language conception, see the classic collection, *The Linguistic Turn: Recent Essays on Philosophical Method*, edited by Richard Rorty (Chicago: University of Chicago Press, 1967).

11   Here I follow the way of putting the matter set out in Ray Monk, *How to Read Wittgenstein*, 68ff.

12   The initial implausiblity of the claim has two sources: the first is Schenker's assertion that musical value (and hence the basis for all judgements of musical value) is a direct function of such tonic-dominant-tonic progressions, the second is the overgeneralization from common-practice tonality to all music as a whole. In fairness to Schenker it is important to note that, if one restricts one's samples to common-practice, and mostly German, music from 1650 to about 1890, the notion that the structural functions of harmony are usually, or often, prolongations of I-V-I progressions is not on its face without plausibility. I owe this point to James Helgeson (to whom I am also indebted for a close and very helpful reading of this essay).

13   By 'roughly speaking', I mean the following: the analogy between the central notion in Chomskian linguistics, that is, deep grammar, and the central notion of Schenkerian analysis, that is, deep tonic-dominant structures, is one that itself calls for a separate and full examination. The question concerning whether there is something analogous to a tonal centre in Chomskian linguistics is instructively difficult: I for one would say that the range of relevancy within a circumstantially-defined subject matter, and the opening and closing of what it is possible or not possible to say within those conversational limits, is such an analogue. But one could I think with some plausibility say that, while music has tonal centres, language does not. (One could also take the term 'tonal' literally here, and consider the limits concerning what is, and what is not, proper tone within a given exchange.) Thanks again to James Helgeson for bringing this question to the forefront.

14   A story is told about Schoenberg that is instructive in this respect: when presented with one of Schenker's graphs (showing by note-size the analysis of foreground and background, or structurally significant and insignificant content respectively), Schoenberg remarked that all his favourite passages were in the tiny — and thus supposedly inessential — notes.

15   Although the linkage I am developing here is to the later and not to the earlier writings of Wittgenstein, I nevertheless have been helped considerably by James K. Wright, *Schoenberg, Wittgenstein, and the Vienna Circle* in this section.

16 Arnold Schoenberg, *Theory of Harmony* (Berkeley: University of California Press, 1983), 309; discussed in Wright, *Schoenberg, Wittgenstein, and the Vienna Circle*, 53.

17 Schoenberg, *Theory of Harmony*, 322–3.

18 In this connection Wright helpfully discusses the famous fourth inversion of the ninth chord in Schoenberg's *Verklärte Nacht*; see Wright, *Schoenberg, Wittgenstein, and the Vienna Circle*, 55 and footnote 159.

19 Schoenberg, *Theory of Harmony*, 323; see again Wright, *Schoenberg, Wittgenstein, and the Vienna Circle*, 55.

20 For a discussion of the central Wittgenstinian notion of the language-game in aesthetic contexts, see my *Meaning and Interpretation: Wittgenstein, Henry James, and Literary Knowledge* (Ithaca: Cornell University Press, 1994), 9–44.

21 *The Glenn Gould Reader*, edited by Tim Page (New York: Alfred A. Knopf, 1984), 136. There is, it should be said, a sense in which what serialism of the kind Gould is discussing here (symmetrical tone rows, for the analytically minded) *implies* is more true to Gould's description than is the actual music as written. That is, the symmetrical rows Gould is describing often generate internal tritones that imply (but do not themselves describe) a triad; it is implied precisely because the ear 'wants' to hear a triad as a resolution of what is heard as the dominant tension within the tritone. This, incidentally, is one of the very many places in musical understanding where what one hears is not reducible to what one, in pure sonic terms, takes in through the auditory system. This is directly linked to, or more strongly is the musical version of, Gricean implicature in the philosophy of language, where what is heard to have been said cannot be reduced to the sum total, and nothing more, of the individual words actually sounded by the speaker. See note 27 below.

22 The rule-following considerations in Wittgenstein's writings have generated a sizeable body of writing in recent decades; one might usefully start with *Wittgenstein: To Follow a Rule*, edited by Steven H. Holtzman and Christopher M. Leich (London: Routledge, 1981). I offer a discussion of the relation (of an often less straightforward kind than one might expect) between applying a rule and rightly understanding in 'Rightness Reconsidered: Krausz, Wittgenstein, and the Question of Interpretive Understanding', in *Interpretation and Ontology: Studies in the Philosophy of Michael Krausz*, edited by A. Deciu and G.L. Pandit (Amsterdam: Rodopi, 2003), 25–37. As we begin to see here, rule following in musical composition and performance is similarly diverse; the model of simple application is far too simple accurately to capture the practices.

23 Wittgenstein's brief and preliminary list in *Philosophical Investigations*, Sec. 23 (offered only as suggestions of a much larger multiplicity) of things we do with (and in) language includes about two dozen. A similar (and similarly long) list could easily be made of compositional types.

24   Arnold Schoenberg, *Style and Idea*, edited by Leonard Stein, translated by Leo Black (Berkeley: University of California Press, 2010, originally published in 1950).

25   Such a reduction can be explicit, and it can be implicitly housed within a set of larger methodological presuppositions. I discuss this in *Describing Ourselves: Wittgenstein and Autobiographical Consciousness*, Chapter 3, 'The Self, Speaking', 76–118. Wittgenstein's writings on what he calls 'an attitude towards a soul' can be seen as antidotes to behavioural reductionism; I offer a reading of *Don Giovanni* in just this light in 'Leporello's Question: *Don Giovanni* as a Tragedy of the Unexamined Life', *Philosophy and Literature* 29:1 (for the Symposium 'Music, Politics, and Morality', April 2005), 180–99.

26   Ludwig Wittgenstein, *Lectures and Conversations on Aesthetics, Psychology, and Religious Belief*, edited by Cyril Barrett (Oxford: Basil Blackwell, 1966), 1.

27   On this point see J.L. Austin, 'The Meaning of a Word', in *Philosophical Papers*, 2nd edition, edited by J.O. Urmson and G.J. Warnock (Oxford: Oxford University Press, 1970), 55–75. The point is developed in the writings of Paul Grice in a way that holds powerful significance for our understanding of musical, and particularly compositional, meaning (but well beyond the scope of the present project); see 'Utterer's Meaning and Intentions', 'Utterer's Meaning, Sentence-Meaning, and Word-Meaning', 'Some Models for Implicature', 'Meaning', and 'Meaning Revisited' in *Studies in the Way of Words* (Cambridge, MA: Harvard University Press, 1989).

28   The reasons an awareness of the complexity of (what is here briefly called) the grammar of imagining is important for aesthetic understanding are themselves somewhat complex: I discuss these in *Art as Language: Wittgenstein, Meaning, and Aesthetic Theory* (Ithaca: Cornell University Press, 1995), Chapter 4, 'Artistic Intention and Mental Image', 75–98.

The Surrealism of the Habitual: From Poetic Language to the Prose of Life

Alison James

Abstract:

This article argues that the later philosophy of Wittgenstein has significant affinities with surrealist approaches to the ordinary. It links the question of ordinary language first to the dilemmas of poetic speech after Mallarmé, then to a current of thought on everyday life that emerges in France in the wake of surrealism (Lefebvre, Blanchot, Certeau). Finally, a reading of prose texts by Breton and Aragon brings together these two lines of argument, demonstrating that surrealism appeals to ordinary language and everyday life as a remedy against the threat of scepticism. Surrealist manipulations of language are less a departure from the real than an attempt both to restore and to renew the human relation with the world. Obscured by its very familiarity, the everyday comes into view as what Cavell calls the 'surrealism of the habitual'.

Keywords: Wittgenstein, Mallarmé, André Breton, Louis Aragon, ordinary language, Stanley Cavell, surrealism

My title is borrowed in part from the philosopher Stanley Cavell, who relates his own view of the ordinary to Heidegger's by stating that both 'respond to the fantastic in what human beings will accustom themselves to, call this the surrealism of the habitual'.[1] In this context, the term 'surrealism' does not refer specifically to the artistic movement of that name, but rather serves as a synonym for strangeness or the uncanny. The 'surrealism of the habitual' is related to a paradox articulated in a number of Cavell's books: namely that the appeal to the ordinary aims to repudiate scepticism, yet contains the sceptical threat within itself.[2] Cavell's work unites literary and philosophical concerns, linking writers, thinkers and poets — Shakespeare, Wordsworth, Coleridge, Emerson, Poe and

Paragraph 34.3 (2011): 406–422
DOI: 10.3366/para.2011.0033
© Edinburgh University Press
www.eupjournals.com/para

others — within a retrospective framework developed from the speech act theory of J. L. Austin and Wittgenstein's *Philosophical Investigations*. Aside from a few cursory mentions, however, the surrealist movement is not one of the 'lines of Romanticism' that holds Cavell's interest.[3] This essay will nevertheless follow Cavell's methodological lead in order to argue that the French surrealists have an important place in this post-Romantic lineage. Surrealism, too, is a quest for the ordinary.

The surrealist writings that I discuss of course predate the publication in 1953 of the *Philosophical Investigations*. The point is not to turn André Breton into an ordinary language philosopher *avant la lettre*. At the most general level, I assume that Wittgenstein's philosophy can have explanatory value for literary uses of language, even if writers offer differing accounts of their own practices. More specifically, I will identify commonalities between surrealist approaches to the everyday and Wittgenstein's account of ordinary language. I am concerned only indirectly with examining the belated French reception of Wittgenstein's philosophy; rather, my approach to 'literary thinking after Cavell after Wittgenstein' (to borrow a phrase from Kenneth Dauber and Walter Jost[4]) relates the question of literary use to the problem of defining and representing the ordinary. In the process, I will connect Wittgenstein's account of ordinary language to the French discourses on 'everyday life' that emerge in the wake of surrealism.

Surrealism and the uses of poetry

Poets need not mean what they say: at first view, this seems to be the central claim of André Breton's 1932 pamphlet *The Poverty of Poetry: The Aragon Affair Before Public Opinion*.[5] The text is Breton's response to the controversy surrounding Aragon's poem 'Red Front', which appeared in the Moscow-based journal *Littérature de la révolution mondiale* in 1931. The poem includes such phrases as 'comrades/Kill the cops' and 'Fire on Leon Blum/Fire on Boncour Froissard Déat/Fire on the trained bears of social democracy'.[6] Aragon was charged with incitement to murder; the surrealists issued a tract ('The Aragon Affair') and a petition defending him on the grounds of the specificity of poetic language.[7] *The Poverty of Poetry* elaborates on this argument, while also attempting to counter the accusation (brought by Communists and others) that the surrealists are taking refuge in the doctrine of art for art's sake.

Far from silencing this last point of criticism, *The Poverty of Poetry* has often been dismissed as an exercise in bad faith.[8] In a

persuasive historical reassessment, Deborah Jenson foregrounds the
intertextual reference to nineteenth-century debates on economics
and metaphysics — Breton's title modifies that of Marx's *The Poverty of
Philosophy* (1847), which itself responds to Proudhon's *The Philosophy of
Poverty* (1846). In Breton's text, Jenson argues, the notion of discursive
poverty reflects the 'vulnerable cultural position' of poetry 'between
the extremes of irrelevance and ideological overdetermination'.[9]
I would like to formulate the problem in different terms: *The Poverty
of Poetry* is an attempt to think through the nature of the poetic speech
act. Close attention to the specific grounds that Breton gives for his
claims allows us to distinguish two lines of argument, one of which
we might characterize as Hegelian/Mallarmean, the other of which is
much closer to Wittgenstein and ordinary language philosophy.

Breton insists that the surrealists are not content to remain mere
spectators of 'the social drama', but also argues that poetry cannot work
as direct political action (*TPP*, 299). He attributes this impossibility
both to the historical situation of poetry (*TPP*, 302) and, more
intrinsically, to its definition: the goal of poetry and art has always
been to soar above the real and above common thought (*TPP*, 299,
303). In formulating this argument, Breton refers to Hegel's lectures
on aesthetics and in particular to Hegel's insistence on the distinction
between poetry and prose.[10] For Hegel, poetry is the most perfect
and most universal of the arts because it comes closest to the self-
apprehension of spirit.[11] However, its linguistic medium poses a
problem, for art 'ought to place us on ground different from that
adopted in our everyday life, as well as in our religious ideas and
actions, and in the speculations of philosophy' (*A* II, 1007). Language,
when used in poetry, should therefore not be left 'in the state in which
it is used every day' (*A* II, 969), but must set itself apart from the
'common prose of life' (*A* I, 245) — an expression that Hegel uses to
refer both to the 'prosaic' dimension of existence and to the linguistic
signs that mediate this level of experience. In this respect, Hegel's
account of poetic language anticipates Mallarmé's famous distinction
between literature and 'universal reporting' (*l'universel reportage*) as well
as other modernist refusals of instrumental language.[12]

Breton mobilizes this conception of poetry both for and against
Aragon's poem. In fact, he does not like 'Red Front', which he
describes as an aesthetically regressive 'poem of circumstance' that
fails to reach beyond the particulars of contemporary public life
(*TPP*, 303). The poem thus occupies a strange middle ground: not
poetic enough to detach itself from current conditions, but too much

of a poem to constitute direct revolutionary action. Nevertheless, Breton asserts that Aragon would not have written the same sentences in a prose essay (*TPP*, 297). He repeats this point in responding to Romain Rolland's objection to the surrealists' defence of Aragon. Refusing to separate writing and action, Rolland had cited a case in which speech had serious repercussions: Charles Maurras's written attacks in *L'Action française* on the French socialist leader Jean Jaurès, which arguably provoked the assassination of Jaurès in 1914. Breton does not dispute Rolland's account of Maurras's acts of incitement, but he insists that the comparison with Aragon's case is nonsensical because it assimilates journalistic and poetic texts (*TPP*, 300).

On a cursory reading, Breton seems to be invoking the 'aesthetic alibi' (a position that should not necessarily be dismissed out of hand).[13] Nevertheless, the most convincing points of his argument depend less on a sharp demarcation between poetic and ordinary language than on the specification of various contextual factors which determine the way in which Aragon's lines function. The criminal charges brought against Aragon are absurd, states Breton, because the poem's apparent acts of incitement simply have no chance of being carried out (*TPP*, 300). Poetic form is one factor since it marks out Aragon's words as a particular kind of speech act. Moreover, the poem must be considered as a whole, which means that we cannot isolate such groups of words as 'kill the cops' from more conventionally lyrical lines such as 'the stars descend familiarly on earth' (*TPP*, 297). The poem must be taken as a unified expression and not a succession of representations (*TPP*, 297–8). What Breton suggests here, in effect, is that there is no clear line between 'literal' and 'metaphorical' meaning when such lines of poetry are read together.

Thus, Breton's ostensibly Hegelian argument might be reformulated in the following Wittgenstinian terms: Aragon's words participate simultaneously in different language games, social, political and poetic, and we need to examine how these games function and overlap. It is not that Aragon's words possess some special poetic property, but that they are used in a particular way. If we recast the claim again in the terminology of speech act theory, we encounter the question of the relationship between illocution and perlocution.[14] First, what is the illocutionary force of Aragon's poem — does it urge readers to kill? Second, what object or sequel does it produce: for instance, convincing the reader to act in a particular way? Breton's argument is of course not formulated in this way, but it does distinguish between the nature of the speech act and its effects. Thus it might be possible, says Breton, to judge a provocation on the basis of its effects, but the main criterion is whether there was an act of provocation in the first place (*TPP*, 300). (As the 'Aragon Affair' itself demonstrates, of course, texts may have unintended consequences: due to complex circumstances, Breton's *The Poverty of Poetry* precipitated a political rupture within surrealism and a personal rupture between Aragon and Breton.)

In *How to Do Things with Words*, J. L. Austin states that in certain kinds of language use there may be no attempt at 'a standard perlocutionary act', 'as Walt Whitman does not seriously incite the eagle of liberty to soar' (*HDTW*, 104). However, the less innocuous example of Aragon's 'Fire on Léon Blum' brings home the inadequacy of Austin's account of poetic speech. It does not seem sufficient to answer that Aragon, in writing an obviously militant poem, is simply not serious. It is no simple matter to determine the illocutionary force of Aragon's problematic lines when we consider their place in the whole poem, as well as the poem's place in a specific historical and poetic context. Aragon's poem celebrates, in terms that are highly metaphorical, the arrival of the 'the train of the red star' (*RF*, 295). Yet to defend the poem in these contextual terms might entail agreeing with Breton's judgement that the close dependence on context diminishes the text's poetic significance. Written during Aragon's stay in the USSR in 1930, 'Red Front' is a poem dictated by circumstances and by what now appears as a misguided political commitment. In his response to the Aragon Affair, Breton attempts to grapple with an important dilemma: surrealism aims to dissolve the boundary between art and life, but it also wants to preserve a space for poetic creation outside ideological commitment, and even outside everyday practice.

Ordinary language, everyday life

While the relation between ordinary and poetic language involves particular quandaries for the avant-garde of the early twentieth century, it is also a perennial question in literary criticism. In recent years, a number of scholars have turned to ordinary language philosophy (sometimes as an alternative to post-structuralist theory).[15] However, as the above discussion of Austin illustrates, ordinary language philosophy has trouble accounting for the literary speech act, except as a form of utterance that is 'parasitic' on 'serious' language use.[16] By contrast with Austin's account, Wittgenstein's description of language as composed of overlapping language-games[17] seems more promising for literary criticism; for one thing, it can be taken to dissolve the notion that literary language is uniquely problematic.[18] Yet some critics have argued that the language-game model, with its pragmatic orientation and its insistence on the given, is inadequate for explaining literary creativity.[19] Does literary language, like metaphysical speculation, remove language from its ordinary use? Does it send language 'on holiday' (*PI*, §38), or can it transform the rules of the game?

'Ordinary language is all right', states Wittgenstein in the *Blue Book*.[20] All right, that is, until philosophers distort it: the task is then, as he puts it in the *Philosophical Investigations*, 'to bring words back from their metaphysical to their everyday use' (*PI*, §116). The preoccupations of modern literature often seem to be quite contrary to Wittgenstein's project. Rather than 'bringing words back', this is a literature that aims to defamiliarize, to make new, to take language and thought away from the commonplace. Nevertheless, some compelling recent work has sought to highlight the place of daily life and the representation of the banal in the literature of European modernism.[21] Focusing specifically on the French context, Michael Sheringham situates surrealism at the beginning of a line of thought on the quotidian that finds its culmination in the post-World War II work of Henri Lefebvre, the Situationists, Roland Barthes, Georges Perec, and Michel de Certeau.[22]

Except in the case of Certeau, as we shall see, the connection between Wittgenstein's appeal to ordinary language and these various attempts to describe, understand or transform everyday life is not immediately obvious. The ordinary for Wittgenstein functions in the first instance as a grammatical limit, rather than as an aspect of reality ('everyday life') to be represented in language; indeed, it entails a critique of the very notion of language as representation. However, it is precisely for this reason that Wittgenstein sheds light on the tension within surrealism between, on the one hand, commitment to renewing poetic language, and on the other hand the attempt to invent a new mode of relation to the everyday. We should be attentive to the fundamental ambiguity of the everyday for both Wittgenstein and the surrealists (this is the 'strangeness of the ordinary' that Marjorie Perloff links to a number of tendencies in contemporary poetics).[23] In developing this line of argument, I follow Cavell's view that Wittgenstein's later philosophy cannot be reduced to an appeal to common sense. Against Austin's assumption that 'both skepticism and metaphysics can be put aside' if we only pay attention to ordinary language (*MWM*, xxi), Cavell emphasizes Wittgenstein's attention to the vulnerability of the ordinary.

Wittgenstein's project presents some striking parallels with French everyday life theory, but also some significant differences. In both cases, the insistence on the value of the ordinary challenges established discourses and disciplines. Wittgenstein's criticism is aimed specifically at philosophical misuses of language. To understand ordinary language is to dissolve the traditional problems of philosophy, 'to show the fly the way out of the fly-bottle' (*PI*, §309). The first volume of Henri Lefebvre's *Critique of Everyday Life*, first published in 1947, opens with a broader attack on both literature and philosophy for their 'great conspiracy' against the everyday life of human beings.[24] Volume Two of Lefebvre's *Critique* (1958) insists on the inadequacy of historical, sociological, philosophical, structuralist, and political approaches to the everyday (*CEL* II, 20–41). Specialized modes of inquiry may be brought to bear on a study of everyday life, but no particular field can properly lay claim to the task of its critique (*CEL* II, 26–7). Indeed, attention to the everyday undermines any such division of knowledge into discrete parcels of reality; for Lefebvre, the critique of everyday life is not a branch of sociology but a 'total critique of totality' (*CEL* II, 27). Both Lefebvre and Wittgenstein are attentive to the question of totality in that they criticize the isolation of particular cases from an understanding of the role they play in our lives (*PI*, §156; *CEL* II, 15). In contrast to Lefebvre's aspiration to a total critique, however, the *Philosophical Investigations* leaves behind the project of a total theory of language of the kind set out in the *Tractatus Logico-Philosophicus*.

Both Lefebvre and Wittgenstein develop a dialogical form of argument that ventriloquizes objections and offers responses. This mode of dialectical inquiry dramatizes the paradoxical difficulty of giving a voice to ordinary language, of hearing the everyday speak. Lefebvre struggles constantly with the problem of defining 'everyday life', repeatedly running up against the impossibility of identifying it with any particular kind of activity (*CEL* II, 41–2). He presents everydayness as a *level* of experience that contains all possibilities of human self-realization, an intermediate and mediating region between the mechanical and the creative, necessity and praxis (*CEL* II, 45–7). Wittgenstein, on the other hand, leaves the ordinary more or less undefined; or rather, the concept of the ordinary takes on meaning within a network of contexts. The adjectives he uses are *gewöhnlich* (ordinary, habitual, customary), *alltäglich* (everyday) and occasionally *normal*; these terms are usually applied to language (sentences, forms of language, language games), sometimes to life (*PI*, §108, §156), and more rarely to distinguish 'ordinary people' (*der gewöhnliche Mensch*) from the metaphysically befuddled philosopher (*PI*, §173). Wittgenstinian 'ordinary language' (*alltägliche Sprache*) is, at the most basic level, simply language that makes sense. Yet in order to separate sense and nonsense, we must grasp the way in which linguistic practices are bound up with a 'form of life' (*PI*, §241).

On the nature and on the adequacy of our forms of life, Wittgenstein has little to say, with the result that he can seem to be preaching acceptance of the given. His emphasis on re-familiarization, on return, on coming home to the everyday, seems very far from Lefebvre's humanist Marxism, with its concern for the distorting effects of capitalism and consumer culture on our language and forms of life. For Lefebvre, everyday life combines current alienation and infinite political potential, and must be simultaneously rehabilitated and criticized before it can be transformed (*CEL* I, 127; II, 18–19). The political implications of Wittgenstein's philosophy are harder to locate. The *Philosophical Investigations* suggest that the source of our estrangement from the everyday runs deeper than the problems of contemporary culture, lying in our tendency to misunderstand the nature of our own language. Terry Eagleton characterizes Wittgenstein's thought as 'numbingly consensual', claiming that it ignores the possibility of disagreement 'between forms of life themselves'.[25] Cavell, by contrast, argues that Wittgenstein's appeal to ordinary language 'does not constitute a defense of ordinary beliefs or common sense', but rather attempts to establish the grounds of our beliefs (*MWM*, 240). Disagreement between forms of life, presumably, becomes possible on this basis.

Perhaps these divergences simply stem from the fact that Wittgenstein deals with ordinary language, Lefebvre with everyday life. In order to bridge the gap between these two perspectives on the ordinary, but also to elucidate the key differences between the Wittgenstinian perspective and the current of French thought that I am exploring, it is helpful to turn to Maurice Blanchot's essay 'Everyday Speech' (1962). Responding to Lefebvre's work, Blanchot argues that undefinability constitutes the very essence of the everyday. The quotidian exists prior to all meaning, and by definition it will always escape the forms and structures that we use to try to comprehend it. The everyday is always already there, always already seen, but precisely for that reason it eludes our understanding.[26] For Blanchot, the realm of the everyday undermines language itself, as well as the conception of the subject. The commonality of the everyday—the fact that it involves shared forms of life — is taken to entail a radical dissolution of subjectivity. Because the everyday belongs to everyone, Blanchot states, it belongs to no one; it can only be the experience of 'anyone at all' (*l'homme quelconque*).[27]

Although there is something Wittgenstinian in the recognition that we will never be able to enclose the quotidian in a 'panoramic vision' (*IC*, 240), Blanchot's attempt to assign an essential negativity to the everyday is very far from the spirit of the *Philosophical Investigations*. (It is perhaps more akin to the *Tractatus*, with its reference to a mystical realm beyond speech.) Blanchot's insistence on a radical opposition between representation and its 'outside' has been extremely influential in shaping recent work on everyday life.[28] The problem, from a Wittgenstinian point of view, is that Blanchot's argument implicitly depends on a representational model of language. If language is understood primarily as a representation of individual thought, then the public, common nature of everyday experience constitutes a threat to both language and representation. In this context (and in a manner characteristic of Blanchot's writing), 'everyday speech' becomes an irreducible paradox: speech without a subject.

Although there is no mention of Wittgenstein in 'Everyday Speech' Blanchot is in fact one of the few French thinkers (along with Pierre Hadot and, a little later, Jacques Bouveresse) to discuss Wittgenstein in the years immediately following Pierre Klossowski's 1961 translation of the *Tractatus* and the *Philosophical Investigations*).[29] In the pages that Blanchot devotes to Wittgenstein, he does not discuss the appeal to ordinary speech. In the 1963 article 'Wittgenstein's Problem', he rather oddly defines Wittgenstein's quandary as the quest for an impossible metalanguage (*IC*, 337).[30] In *The Writing of the Disaster* (1980), he describes the *Philosophical Investigations* as an attempt to purify reason by preserving it from the fascination of literary language.[31] Ultimately, we might see Blanchot's work as the supreme example of something Wittgenstein warns about: the human capacity to find dizzying metaphysical depths in the most ordinary things. For Cavell, this capacity is one of the sources of scepticism.

A more successful encounter with Wittgenstein takes place in Michel de Certeau's work on the everyday. In particular, Certeau is drawn to the problem raised by the concluding sections of the *Tractatus*: the question of the limits of language and world. At the same time, he comes closer than Blanchot to the Wittgenstein of the *Philosophical Investigations*. In *The Practice of Everyday Life* (1980), Certeau draws on Wittgenstein's account of ordinary language in order to develop a description of the tactical creativity of everyday practices (walking, shopping, cooking). For Certeau, Wittgenstein reveals the possibility of an approach to everyday life that does not depend on seeking grounds outside the ordinary.[32] Following Wittgenstein, Certeau accepts that we cannot find a position outside ordinary language from which to describe it. Unlike Blanchot, he does not turn this absence of an 'outside' into an essential metaphysical lack. It is a limit within which we must function: 'We are subject to, but not identified with, ordinary language. As in the ship of fools, we are embarked, without the possibility of an aerial view or any sort of totalization. That is the "prose of the world" Merleau-Ponty spoke of' (*PEL*, 11).

The prose of the world

Certeau's reference to Merleau-Ponty introduces an unexpected connection between Wittgenstein and Hegel, via French phenomenology. 'The prose of the world', is Hegel's expression before it is taken up by Merleau-Ponty. In Hegel, as we have seen, it takes on a largely negative sense: the prose of the world or the prose of life is 'the prose of finitude and commonplace thinking', which art and the beautiful transcend in order to reach an intermediary realm between the 'sensuous sphere' and 'the higher spheres of religion and philosophy' (*A* II, 968). Merleau-Ponty's unfinished book *The Prose of the World* (1969) reverses Hegel's hierarchy in that the object of human aspiration is now the realm of the concrete, the world of things.[33] Nevertheless, Merleau-Ponty believes with Hegel that both poetry and great prose can transcend the merely prosaic (*PW*, 63). Creative language, or, in Merleau-Ponty's terms, speech or 'speaking language' (*langage parlant*) leads us back to the world by displacing and decentering the meanings of 'sedimented language' (*langage parlé*) (*PW*, 10–20, 16–22). If this view of language sounds quite unlike Wittgenstein's, Michel de Certeau nevertheless points the way to a reconciliation of the two perspectives: creative language does not leap outside ordinary language-games, but opens up a space for the new through a tactical engagement with the given.

I began this study by positioning Breton's views on poetry and language between Wittgenstein and Hegel — that is, between an acknowledged influence (Hegel) and a very different kind of philosopher whose potential affinities with surrealism emerge in retrospect. In referring to Hegel, Breton implicitly calls into question the value of ordinary forms of life and language, understood as the realm of the prosaic. Yet, as some have pointed out, Hegel's hostility to the immediate is incompatible with the surrealist project.[34] Commitment to the ordinary underwrites the surrealists' development of forms of writing that, contrary to Hegelian precepts, do not clearly demarcate themselves from the 'prose of the world' or from other spheres of discourse. This is why Walter Benjamin states: 'the writings of this circle are not literature but something else — demonstrations, watchwords, documents, bluffs, forgeries if you will, but at any rate not literature.'[35] This is no doubt to overstate the case, and yet it seems an apt description of certain surrealist prose texts: Aragon's *Paris Peasant* (1926) and Breton's quartet — *Nadja* (1928), *Communicating Vessels* (1932), *Mad Love,* (1937) and *Arcane 17* (1944). We read these as literary works, certainly, but they are also documents 'taken from life' ('pris sur le vif'), as Breton says of *Nadja*,[36] as well as philosophical meditations overwhelmingly concerned with problems of perception, knowledge and doubt.

The ambiguity of the surrealist everyday can be linked to the imprecision of the term 'surréalisme' itself. In his 1924 manifesto, Breton relates the term to the 'superior reality' of certain types of association (*OC* I, 328), but he insists in *What is Surrealism?* (1934) that the word expresses the desire to apprehend the world perceived by the senses ('le monde sensible') (*OC* II, 231). This ambiguity can be related to Wittgenstein's comment that it is no simple matter to 'look and see' how ordinary language is used: 'The aspects of things that are most important for us are hidden because of their simplicity and familiarity. (One is unable to notice something — because it is always before one's eyes)' (*PI*, §129). It is this aspect of Wittgenstein's philosophy that leads Cavell to argue that metaphysics cannot easily be set aside in favour of the ordinary, that in the *Philosophical Investigations* 'the voices of melancholy and merriment, or of metaphysics and the ordinary (. . .), are caused by one another, and form an argument that is not to be decided but is to be dismantled.'[37] Wittgenstein's sense of the ordinary, for Cavell, can be connected to a Romantic tradition that responds to a form of modern scepticism rooted in Kant's epistemology. The literary and philosophical quest for the ordinary responds to the disappointment of what Cavell calls the 'Kantian settlement', the compromise which grounds human knowledge of the world only by putting the 'thing in itself' out of our reach (*QO*, 4). For Cavell, the devotion to the ordinary, the familiar, and the common 'speaks to an intimacy with existence and of an intimacy lost, that matches scepticism's despair of the world' (*QO*, 31–2).

In *Paris Peasant*, Aragon's attempts at exhaustive description aim towards an impossible remedy for the anguished sense that the world is never accessible; they aim to break through the Kantian limits on understanding:

I do not subscribe to the view that the world can be had for the asking. This handkerchief saleswoman, this little sugar bowl which I will describe to you if you don't behave yourself, are interior boundaries of myself, ideal views I have of my laws, of my ways of thought, and may I be strung up by the neck if this passage is anything else but a method of freeing myself of certain inhibitions, a means of obtaining access to a hitherto forbidden realm that lies beyond my human energies.[38]

In his quest for a metaphysics of the concrete, Aragon turns to Hegel in preference to Kant. However, the world remains out of reach: 'The concrete is the indescribable; why should I care two pins whether the earth is round or not?' (*PP*, 205).[39] A partial solution lies in the surrealist image, which presents itself as an immediate fact. The image, says Aragon, does not coincide with the concrete; it nevertheless offers the greatest possible consciousness of the concrete (*PP*, 201). It has become a critical commonplace, from Benjamin onwards, to blame Aragon for remaining in the realm of dreams and seeking escape from the everyday in the realm of the marvellous.[40] However, this is unfairly to deflate the central stakes of *Paris Peasant*. Aragon appeals to the everyday, the concrete and the factual in order to confront and strive to overcome what Cavell calls scepticism's 'despair of the world.' This is the threat that hangs over *Paris Peasant*—everything is crumbling under my gaze (*PP*, 48)[41]—and which is only matched by the text's poetic exuberance, humour and descriptive vitality. Despair itself even takes a comic turn in the appearance of the personified 'Sense of the useless', carrying the accordion of pessimism (*PP*, 48–9).

Cavell argues that ordinary language philosophy 'is not a defence of what may present itself as certain fundamental, cherished beliefs about the world and the creatures in it, but, among other things, a contesting of that presentation, for, as it were, the prize of the ordinary' (*QO*, 4). While Aragon's *Paris Peasant* both dramatizes and deflates scepticism's threat to this prize of the ordinary, Breton's prose texts are more optimistic in their turn away from scepticism. In one anecdote of *Communicating Vessels*, Breton accompanies a girl to a charcuterie to buy some gherkins, and finds himself, in contemplating the pleasure of eating these pickles, suddenly reconciled with everyday life.[42] Breton's main subject in this text is the fundamental continuity between dreams and waking life, but his approach does not involve the simple unification or *Aufhebung* of the two states, as his second surrealist manifesto had seemed to suggest (*OC* I, 781). Although

Communicating Vessels seeks to demonstrate the continuity of desire in both states of consciousness, Breton emphatically rejects the sceptical version of the problem of dreams; that is, the question of whether waking life might itself be a dream. This is simply nonsense, states Breton, and illustrates his point with an analogy: 'Would we not be equally justified in decreeing, because drunks see double, that for the eyes of a sober man the repetition of an object is the consequence of *a slightly different* drunkenness? As this difference would result from the material fact of *having drunk or not having drunk*, I consider it useless to insist further' (*CV*, 107).[43] Here — we are once again in 1932 — Breton is clearly trying to present himself as a good materialist. Yet the comparison also sounds rather Wittgenstinian, in that it describes the philosopher's dilemma as an odd misuse of language. We can be sceptics, Breton suggests, only by ignoring the way in which the words 'dream' and 'drunkenness' are normally used.

Wittgenstein asserts that 'My *life* consists in my being content to accept many things.' Belief always comes before doubt, and individual beliefs are inseparable from a larger world-picture and language-game.[44] For Breton, however, this acceptance cannot be the end of the story. He points out that it is possible to function more or less normally as an embodied creature in the everyday world — avoiding being run over by cars in the street, for example (*CV*, 106) — while still facing an urgent need to reconstitute a sense of self. This problem of the relation of self and world, is at the heart of Breton's prose cycle, beginning with the question 'Who am I?' ('Qui suis-je?') that opens *Nadja* (*OC* I, 646). Breton's position has close affinities with Cavell's, in that it recasts epistemological doubt as essentially a problem of self-knowledge and of our relation to others. There is a truth of scepticism, for Cavell, insofar as 'our relation to the world as a whole, or to others in general, is not one of knowing, where knowing construes itself as being certain'.[45] In this context, Breton's famous and much derided notions of 'objective chance' and 'mad love', might be said to function as modes of what Cavell calls 'acknowledgement'. This is a form of engagement with the world and with others. It responds to the threat of scepticism and solipsism, not by refuting the sceptical challenge but by displacing the problem (*QO*, 8–9).

The surrealist movement 'was born as a far-reaching operation having to do with language' states Breton in the 1953 essay 'On Surrealism in Its Living Works'.[46] Surrealism is concerned in a very literal sense with language-games and with language as game. The manipulation of ordinary ways of saying is a means of contesting established ways of seeing. Nevertheless, in an important sense surrealism starts from a position of faith in ordinary language — 'I know what all my words mean and syntax comes to me *naturally*', states Breton in his 'Introduction to the Discourse on the Paucity of Reality' (1927).[47] The naturalness of what Cavell calls the 'human habitat' (*QO*, 149) appears in surrealism as something yet to be discovered. 'Existence is elsewhere' is the phrase that concludes Breton's 1924 manifesto (MS, 47), while the closing section of *Communicating Vessels* argues that the abolition of class differences would simply create the conditions for all people to confront the real questions about human existence: 'It is, I think, too simple to want to reduce man's need for some adequation to life to a painful reflex which would be likely to cede to the suppression of classes' (*CV*, 140).[48] In 1953, Breton speaks of returning the degraded language of the modern world to a previous state, of restoring language to its true life (*MS*, 298). While the surrealist writer thus appears as an unexpected philosopher of the ordinary, Wittgenstein in turn is alert to the surreal dimension of everyday life in the modern world: 'ordinary common sense' he asserts in a note of 1937, 'no longer suffices to meet the strange demands life makes.'[49] Ultimately, Breton and Wittgenstein have in common the belief that we live in exile from our words, and both take on the surprisingly difficult task of seeking a home in the ordinary world.

NOTES

1 Stanley Cavell, *In Quest of the Ordinary: Lines of Skepticism and Romanticism* (Chicago: University of Chicago Press, 1988), 154, henceforward *QO*.

2 Stanley Cavell, *Must We Mean What We Say?*, updated edition (Cambridge: Cambridge University Press, (1969), 2002), 238–66, henceforward *MWM*.

3 See Stanley Cavell, *The World Viewed: Reflections on the Ontology of Film*, revised edition (Cambridge, MA: Harvard University Press, 1979), 95, 96, 108, 233 n. 21; *MWM*, 131.

4 *Ordinary Language Criticism: Literary Thinking After Cavell After Wittgenstein*, edited by Kenneth Dauber and Walter Jost (Evanston, IL: Northwestern University Press, 2003).

5 André Breton, *The Poverty of Poetry: The Aragon Affair before Public Opinion*, in Maurice Nadeau, *History of Surrealism*, translated by Richard Howard (New York: Macmillan, 1965), 296–303. Henceforward *TPP*.

6 Louis Aragon, 'Red Front', in Nadeau, *The History of Surrealism*, 285–95 (287–8), henceforward *RF*. 'Camarades/descendez les flics'; 'Feu sur Léon Blum/Feu sur Boncour Froissard Déat/Feu sur les ours savants de la social-démocratie', Aragon, *Œuvres poétiques complètes*, edited by Olivier

Barbarant (Paris: Gallimard, Bibliothèque de la Pléiade, 2007), I, 495–6, henceforward *OPC*.

7   See Olivier Barbarant's 'Notice' for Aragon's *Persécuté persécuteur, OPC* I, 1361.

8   Jean-Paul Sartre, 'Qu'est-ce que la littérature?', *Situations* II (Paris: Gallimard, 1948), 325; Roger Shattuck, 'The Poetics of Revolution', *The Bulletin of the Midwest Modern Language Association* 2 (1969), 67–76 (73).

9   Deborah Jenson, *Trauma and its Representations: The Social Life of Mimesis in Post-Revolutionary France* (Baltimore: Johns Hopkins University Press, 2001), 144–5.

10 The lessons on aesthetics were the first of Hegel's works to appear in French, in the translation by Charles-Magloire Bénard (5 volumes, 1840–1852; followed by a two-volume version in 1855). See Michael P. Kelly, *Hegel in France* (Birmingham: Birmingham Modern Languages Publications, 1992), 6.

11 G.W.F. Hegel, *Aesthetics: Lectures on Fine Art*, translated by T. M. Knox, 2 vols (Oxford: Clarendon Press, 1988), II, 960, henceforward *A* I or *A* II.

12 Stéphane Mallarmé, 'Crise de vers', in *Oeuvres complètes*, edited by Bertrand Marchal, 2 vols (Paris: Gallimard, Bibliothèque de la Pléiade, 1998–2003), II, 212–3.

13 On this point see Martin Jay, 'The Aesthetic Alibi', *Salmagundi* 93 (1992); reprinted in *The New Salmagundi Reader*, edited by Robert Boyers and Peggy Boyers (Syracuse, NY: Syracuse University Press, 1996), 294–305.

14 J.L. Austin, *How to Do Things with Words* (Cambridge, MA: Harvard University Press, 1962), 117–8, henceforward *HDTW*.

15 Dauber and Jost, Introduction, *Ordinary Language Criticism*, xi.

16 The distinction between 'serious' and 'parasitic' speech acts is one of the central questions of the Derrida–Searle debate of 1977. See Jacques Derrida, *Limited Inc.* (Evanston, IL: Northwestern University Press, 1988); John Searle, '*Reiterating the differences*', *Glyph* 1 (1977), 198–208.

17 Ludwig Wittgenstein, *Philosophical Investigations*, translated by G. E. M. Anscombe, 3rd edition (Oxford: Blackwell, 2001), §7, henceforward *PI*.

18 Charles Altieri, 'Wittgenstein on Consciousness and Language: A Challenge to Derridean Literary Theory', *MLN* 91:6 (December 1976), 1397–1423 (1414).

19 See James Noggle, 'The Wittgenstinian Sublime', *New Literary History* 27:4 (1996), 605–19; Christopher Lawn, 'Gadamer on Poetic and Everyday Language', *Philosophy and Literature* 25 (2001), 113–26.

20 Ludwig Wittgenstein, *Preliminary Studies for 'The Philosophical Investigations', generally known as The Blue and Brown Books* (New York: Harper & Row, 1958), 28.

21 See especially Liesl Olson, *Modernism and the Ordinary* (New York: Oxford University Press, 2009).

22 Michael Sheringham, *Everyday Life: Theories and Practices from Surrealism to the Present* (Oxford: Oxford University Press, 2006), henceforward *EL*.

23 Marjorie Perloff, *Wittgenstein's Ladder: Poetic Language and the Strangeness of the Ordinary* (Chicago: University of Chicago Press, 1996).

24 Henri Lefebvre, *Critique of Everyday Life*, volumes I and II, translated by John Moore (London: Verso, 1991 and 2002), I, 127; henceforward *CEL* I or *CEL* II.

25 Terry Eagleton, 'Wittgenstein's Friends', in *Against the Grain: Essays 1975–1985* (London: Verso, 1986), 121.

26 Maurice Blanchot, *The Infinite Conversation*, translated by Susan Hanson (Minneapolis and London: University of Minnesota Press, 1993), 238–45 (239–40), henceforward *IC*.

27 Maurice Blanchot, *L'Entretien infini* (Paris: Gallimard, 1969), 364, henceforward *EI*.

28 Michael E. Gardiner, *Critiques of Everyday Life* (London: Routledge, 2000), 12, 16; Ben Highmore, *Everyday Life and Cultural Theory: An Introduction* (New York: Routledge, 2002), 1, 20–21; Sheringham, *EL*, 16–22.

29 See Christian Delacampagne, 'Jacques Bouveresse' in *The Columbia History of Twentieth-Century French Thought*, edited by Lawrence D. Kritzman (New York: Columbia University Press, 2006), 447–9 (448).

30 See Wittgenstein, 'One might think: if philosophy speaks of the use of the word "philosophy" there must be a second-order philosophy. But it is not so: it is, rather, like the case of orthography, which deals with the word 'orthography' among others without then being second-order' (*PI*, §121).

31 Maurice Blanchot, *The Writing of the Disaster*, translated by Ann Smock (Lincoln, NE: University of Nebraska Press, 1995), 132.

32 Michel de Certeau, *The Practice of Everyday Life*, translated by Steven Rendall (Berkeley and Los Angeles: University of California Press, 2002), 9–10, henceforward *PEL*. On Certeau, Wittgenstein, and Cavell see also Sheringham, *EL*, 227–33.

33 Maurice Merleau-Ponty, *The Prose of the World*, edited by Claude Lefort, translated by John O'Neill (Evanston, IL: Northwestern University Press, 1973), 4, henceforward *PW*.

34 Ferdinand Alquié, *Philosophie du surréalisme* (Paris: Flammarion, 1955), 60–1; Blanchot, 'Thought and the Exigency of Discontinuity' (*IC*, 9).

35 Walter Benjamin, 'Surrealism: Last Snapshot of the European Intelligentsia' (1929), in *Selected Writings, Volume 2: 1927–1934*, edited by Michael W. Jennings, Howard Eiland, and Gary Smith, translated by Rodney Livingstone (Cambridge, MA: Belknap Press, 1999), 208.

36 André Breton, *Nadja*, in *Œuvres complètes*, edited by Marguerite Bonnet, 4 vols (Paris: Gallimard, Bibliothèque de la Pléiade, 1988–2008), vol. I, 646. Henceforward *OC* I, II, III, or IV.

37 Stanley Cavell, 'Notes and Afterthoughts on the Opening of Wittgenstein's *Investigations*', in *The Cambridge Companion to Wittgenstein*, edited by Hans Sluga and David G. Stern (Cambridge: Cambridge University Press, 1996), 270.

38 Louis Aragon, *Paris Peasant*, translated by Simon Watson Taylor (Boston: Exact Change, 1994), 88, henceforward *PP*. 'Que le monde m'est donné, ce n'est pas mon sentiment. Cette marchande de mouchoirs, ce petit sucrier que je vais vous décrire si vous n'êtes pas sages, ce sont des limites intérieures de moi-même, des vues idéales que j'ai de mes lois, de mes façons de penser, et je veux bien être pendu si ce passage est autre chose qu'une méthode pour m'affranchir de certaines contraintes, un moyen d'accéder au-delà de mes forces à un domaine encore interdit' (*OPC* I, 207–8).

39 'Le concret, c'est l'indescriptible: à savoir si la terre est ronde, que voulez-vous que ça me fasse?' (*OPC* I, 295).

40 Walter Benjamin, *The Arcades Project* (Cambridge, MA: Harvard University Press, 2002), 458, 464, 908; Sheringham, *EL*, 77–8.

41 'Tout se détruit sous ma contemplation' (*OPC*, I, 177).

42 André Breton, *Communicating Vessels*, translated by Mary Ann Caws and Geoffrey T. Harris (Lincoln: University of Nebraska Press, 1990), 79, henceforward *CV*.

43 'Ne serait-on pas aussi fondé, parce que les ivrognes voient double, à décréter que pour l'œil d'un homme sobre, la répétition d'un objet est la conséquence d'une ivresse *un peu différente*? Comme cette différence résulterait du fait matériel d'*avoir bu* ou de *ne pas avoir bu*, j'estime qu'il n'y a pas lieu d'insister' (*OC* II, 180).

44 Ludwig Wittgenstein, *On Certainty,* edited by G. E. M. Anscombe and G. H. von Wright, translated by Denis Paul and G. E. M. Anscombe (New York: Harper & Row, 1972), §344; §160, §167, §283.

45 Stanley Cavell, *The Claim of Reason: Wittgenstein, Skepticism, Morality and Tragedy*, (New York and Oxford: Oxford University Press, (1979) 1999), 45.

46 André Breton, *Manifestoes of Surrealism*, translated by Richard Seaver and Helen R. Lane (Ann Arbor: University of Michigan Press, 1972), 297, henceforward *MS*. 'Le surréalisme (...) a pris naissance dans une opération de grande envergure portant sur le langage' (*OC* IV, 19).

47 André Breton, 'Introduction to the Discourse on the Paucity of Reality', translated by Richard Sieburth and Jennifer Gordon, October 69 (1994): 133–44. 'Je sais le sens de tous mes mots et j'observe *naturellement* la syntaxe' (*OC* II, 275).

48 'Il est trop simple, selon moi, de vouloir réduire le besoin d'adéquation de l'homme à la vie à un réflexe pénible qui aurait chance de céder à la suppression des classes' (*OC* II, 203).

49 Ludwig Wittgenstein, *Culture and Value* (Chicago: University of Chicago Press, 1984), 27.

Wittgenstein in Recent French Poetics: Henri Meschonnic and Jacques Roubaud

MARIA RUSANDA MURESAN

Abstract:

Two recent French poets, Henri Meschonnic and Jacques Roubaud, have found in Wittgenstein's philosophy an alternative to post-structuralist poetics. Meschonnic's poetry and his theoretical writings show a sustained critical engagement with Wittgenstein, whom he reads in conjunction with Emile Benveniste. The writers inform his theory of poetic rhythm and his practice of biblical translation. Roubaud's use of Wittgenstein, by contrast, here examined in the collection *Quelque chose noir* (1984), is linked partly with the poet's grief following the death of his wife Alix Cléo Roubaud, a photographer and an avid reader of Wittgenstein. In Roubaud, Wittgenstein opens up the space for a meditation on disappearance and absence. Roubaud reformulates passages from Wittgenstein's *On Certainty* (Wittgenstein's last philosophical text written when he was already seriously ill) in poems evoking Alix's memory.

Keywords: Wittgenstein, Henri Meschonnic, Jacques Roubaud, rhythm, poetics, death, mourning, certainty

In the 1970s and 1980s, two prominent French poets, Henri Meschonnic and Jacques Roubaud, engaged with the totality of Wittgenstein's philosophy, from the early *Tractatus Logico-Philosophicus* to the late *On Certainty*, in conceptualizing poetic practice and as a source of poetic material. I examine the terms, and the consequences, of this engagement here.

Paragraph 34.3 (2011): 423–440
DOI: 10.3366/para.2011.0034
© Edinburgh University Press
www.eupjournals.com/para

A poetics of rhythm: Henri Meschonnic

The first French poet to offer a serious account of Wittgenstein's work from the perspective of poetry is Henri Meschonnic, in a 1978 chapter entitled 'Wittgenstein: language philosophy and poetry'.[1] Wittgenstein's entire oeuvre, from the *Tractatus* to the *Philosophical Investigations*, is there analysed for its 'implications for poetics, which is to say not necessarily their explicit or implicit poetics'.[2] Wittgenstein had appeared in Meschonnic's writings as early as 1973, when the poet had noted connections between Wittgenstein's project and his own, in particular the need to 'displace the notion of the unsayable, the ineffable'.[3] In 1978, these traits would become the basis of his disagreement with Wittgenstein's philosophy, in particular, what Meschonnic understood as the philosopher's implicit theories of silence, signs and metalanguage.

Meschonnic welcomes Wittgenstein's demonstration of the fundamental link between what one says, how one says it and the way one lives. He quotes Wittgenstein extensively, both the *Tractatus* and the *Investigations*, and admires the philosopher's close attention to specific concrete linguistic practices as opposed to general claims. Yet he suggests that by using the philosophical theme of what cannot be said but only shown, Wittgenstein maintains the Western metaphysical paradigm of the sign, evident in particular in Wittgenstein's mystical evocation of silence to thwart propositions that are not signs of fact. He critiques Wittgenstein's theory of language for conferring value to silence. For Meschonnic, value cannot be assigned to silence as such, but only to the poem's transformation of silence into language; indeed, this is Meschonnic's own approach to poetry.

These critiques seem surprising, as we know that the later Wittgenstein undermines the idea that language can be understood from within a theory of the sign. Wittgenstein aimed to offer us a *synoptic view* of the ways in which ordinary language functions. His method uncovers apparently 'correct' sentences that run idle, having no real function in life. Wittgenstein explains the pervasive role of the sign in our life in developmental terms: linking words to things has been the main technique of teaching a new language, but it is only a preliminary activity in the process of the acquisition of real uses of our ordinary language. For Wittgenstein the 'theory of the sign' is a reparative 'game', used in cases in which the actual function of language is not 'mastered' by the speaker. Such cases characterize the acquisition of our native tongue or of any foreign language. Certainly these idle sentences are, for Meschonnic, the main tenets of a 'theory of the sign'; indeed the theory of the sign appears, in Meschonnic, as the source of the most 'non-functional' sentences of our ordinary language.

Wittgenstein's attachment to these units of language — 'word' and 'sentence' —, as if to a 'ladder' one might kick away when it is no longer useful, remains a mystery for Meschonnic; indeed, Wittgenstein's critique of the sign is not radical enough for the poet, who critiques the habit of taking word or sentence (*énoncé*) as the main constituents of language practices. As a consequence of his failure to displace the 'theory of the sign' by maintaining the sentence as a unit of analysis, Wittgenstein fails as well, for Meschonnic, to offer a satisfactory theory of the subject in language, essential to the theorization of poetry. He charges Wittgenstein with a reduction of the subject in language to the semantics of psychological expressions: e.g. 'I am in pain', 'I see' 'I know', 'I believe', 'I remember', 'I interpret', 'I understand'. For the French poet, the grammatical difference between the expressive mode of the 'I' and the 'descriptive' mode of the 'he/she' cannot account for the complex functioning of the 'subject of language', which depends on other factors as well, such as prosody and rhythm.

Meschonnic's critique also turns against the relationship between language and metalanguage, that is, against Wittgenstein's rejection of what might be called 'theory' ('Philosophy is not a theory, but an activity').[4] He polemically articulates his own 'theory' with a specific practice of language, a theory that he calls, in the 1970s, an *epistemology of writing*, and in 1980s, an *anthropology of rhythm*. To understand these points of contention between a radical critic such as Meschonnic and a radical philosopher such as Wittgenstein, one should be able to measure the distance between their intellectual projects: the redefinition of the role of philosophy as a humanistic discipline, which is Wittgenstein's endeavour, and the effort to open a space for a new discipline, the anthropology of rhythm, which is Meschonnic's struggle. Their fundamental dissimilarity is a result of their different fields of intervention as well as the history of their disciplines within humanistic inquiry.

Wittgenstein's critique centres on the status of philosophy, which has become a 'theory' no longer in touch with any form of life. Meschonnic's theses originate in a situation similar to that envisioned by Wittgenstein: he starts from the fact that the contemporary institution of literature is a theory no longer embedded in a real form of life shaped by poetic language. While in all other disciplines professors of philosophy or scientists are themselves philosophers or scientists to various degrees, most literary theorists are not poets, novelists or translators of literary texts. Thus, for Meschonnic, literary theory is made of claims and even slogans that do not reflect the actual practice of the reading or writing of poems.[5] Yet, unlike Wittgenstein, who is suspicious of metaphilosophy, for Meschonnic a metadiscourse is necessary, to make manifest the reflective function present in any practice of poetry. Thus he attacks what he considers idle theories of literature without abandoning the project of a theory of poetry.

For Wittgenstein, in the *Philosophical Investigations*, the philosopher does not intervene through/in a 'philosophical discourse', but through what he calls an assembling of reminders (*Erinnerungen*) which are 'statements about' (*Aussagen*) phenomena, and not the phenomena themselves. This operation is described as a comparison (*Gleichnis* = parable; *Gleichung* = equation, see *TLP* 4.241) of pictures (*Bilder*) opposed to deduction and explanation. The statements are compared in such a way as to change one's vision of things:

But was I trying to draw someone's attention to the fact that he is capable of imagining that? — I wanted to put that picture before him, and his *acceptance* of the picture consists in his now being inclined to regard a given case differently: that is, to compare it (*vergleichen*) with *this* rather than *that* set of pictures. I have changed his *way of looking at things* (*Auschauungsweise*).[6]

For Wittgenstein, philosophy does not discover anything new. On the contrary, it precedes all 'discovery' (scientific or empirical). At the same time it aims at a radical change elsewhere, on the level of our vision of the world. French philosophers have attempted to resolve his apparent paradox either by aligning Wittgenstein's thought with a philosophy of the subject that proposes a continuous or punctual conversion[7] or by considering it *an anti-philosophy* for which action alone has to counteract the claim that everything is thinkable.[8] While such philosophers focus on the 'possible' in Wittgenstein's philosophy, as 'sayable', 'thinkable', or 'doable', in order to understand this change, Meschonnic will come to terms with it by focusing on 'actual statements' and the way in which they function in the *Tractatus*, the *Blue and Brown Books* and the *Philosophical Investigations*.

When we focus on the statements that Wittgenstein chooses to analyse, what is not apparent are the ways in which the 'statements' – 'reminders' are selected. Wittgenstein mentions Augustine's *Confessions* as a series of such 'statements' – 'reminders' (*PI*, § 90) — about phenomena. This is what Meschonnic would contest, and this is also the centre of his critique of Wittgenstein. Meschonnic claims that a new unity of language, irreducible to statement alone, is essential to human existence. He calls this unit, discourse (*discours*), and the feature that exceeds the assemblage of statements, rhythm. The key element here is the notion of comparison. Meschonnic would say that Augustine's *Confessions* is a discourse, which is a unit of language where meaning exceeds the 'sum' of its statements, and thus it would not allow these statements to create comparisons as they do in ordinary life. Discourse orients comparison, so that some statements in a discourse can be used in comparison, others not, depending on how other elements of the discourse, such as sound and syntax, correlate. In order to explain the split between the theory and practice of poetry, he unfolds a complex historical argument over several books (*Pour une poétique*, II–V), which can be read as prolegomena to his two books on rhythm: *Critique du rythme* and *Politique du rythme*.[9] The chapter on Wittgenstein is part of this historical argument, which consists of the critical analysis of major Western philosophical and poetic discourses (i.e. Saussure, Humboldt, Hegel, structuralism, Tel Quel, Derrida and so forth) from the point of view of their implications for a theory of poetry and poetics. In this view, the main tenets of all Western theory about the relationship between language and life remained unchanged throughout history and can be described by what he calls a *theory of the sign*. Language activity in the world has always been reduced in a form or another to the link between words and things, where the word is a sign of a thing (be it an object, matter of fact, or more abstract entity).

The theory of the sign has three main consequences. While it proclaims the essential separation of things from words (a sign points to the absence of a thing), by the same token it produces the need of a compensatory function of language that overcomes this gap, that makes the things speak and that manifests their presence. It is one part of Meschonnic's historical demonstration to show how all Western philosophies and theories of language have assigned this compensatory function to poetry.[10] Poetry is thus kept outside ordinary language, and all theories of poetry become a celebration of its reparatory and compensatory function with no real cognitive content. Second, the theory of the sign entails generalizations from a limited number of language units to the entire language. Third, it fails to explain the historicity of language, present as effects of memorability, longevity, of certain discourses as compared to the transience of others. The theory of the sign can only compare and describe how different words are linked to different things over time, but it fails to build an argument as to why certain sequences continue to speak regardless of the things they are linked to, while others disappear entirely from 'use'. Meschonnic's working hypothesis is that the theory of the sign can be invalidated, if poetics departs entirely from an analytics of word meaning, word use, word composition, and is founded in the notion of discourse.

Meschonnic's immediate reference for the notion of discourse is Emile Benveniste in his *Problèmes de linguistique générale*. He starts from Benveniste's theory in which language is essentially the enunciation (*énonciation*) of the subject, and not a statement (*énoncé*) 'about' things. Benveniste works out an intuition similar to that we find at work in Wittgenstein's *Tractatus*: the subject's will is effaced from the language used to describe the world of facts. Benveniste's treatment of the subject springs from his treatment of the tense system in French according to two distinct and complementary systems. Both are in concurrent use and remain available for each reader. These two systems make manifest two different planes of enunciation, which we will distinguish as the plane of "story" (*histoire*) and that of discourse (*discours*).[11] The subject is present in discourse, while it is effaced in the story.[12]

Meschonnic explores this theory of discourse on a new plane: he transforms Benveniste's theory of inter-subjective interaction into an investigation of the dialectics between writing and reading, creation and reception. There is in this search for a description of rhythm something very close to Wittgenstein's *Philosophical Investigations*. In a series of books that might be considered his 'poetical investigations', Meschonnic makes us see rhythm in all its functional diversity, in the same way in which Wittgenstein criticized the supposed uniformity of 'meaning' in language. Meschonnic considers that 'use', as it appears in the *Philosophical Investigations*, lays bare language activity and its full power as an action through/of words on things. Unlike in Wittgenstein, language as discourse (and not as statement) is a transformation of the subject, not of things in the world. Poetic discourse is most exemplary in this sense: poetry is a *direct* organization of the subject, in the relationship between the individual subject and society, while it remains an *indirect* action on things, as a consequence of the reorientation of the subject in the world. Through rhythm poetry rises above a direct action on things. One feels language as use, not word use, as soon as one perceives a voice within a discourse. When we cannot perceive this voice, we say that the language is dead.

This original mixture of Benveniste (*discours*) and Wittgenstein, borrowing as well from Gerard Manley Hopkins's concept of 'sprung rhythm', takes place under the pressure of a very particular practice in language, fundamental to Meschonnic's career as a poet and theorist: the translation of the Bible. It is through this practice that Meschonnic sets the relationship between poetic language and ordinary language. When translating these ancient Hebrew texts Meschonnic wanted to keep all poetic effects present, while at the same time emphasizing the natural cadence of the French ordinary idiom against 'translation French'.[13] For Meschonnic, previous translations departed from this imperative, because they understood the Hebrew language as the sacred language of scriptures and preserved only the literal meaning and value of each word or grammatical structure in the text. Opposing literality, Meschonnic finds the poetry in the biblical texts, in an idiom that makes them interesting for us today, which resides in a system of contrasts in the verb tenses that are created differently in each text, as well as in the non-metrical rhythm of the text, which organizes it as the real movement of speech. Meschonnic also discovers that a translation that foregrounds the story at the expense of discourse fails to account for the most important trait of the Biblical narrative, which is speech and rhythm.[14] Poetry is in direct continuity with ordinary language inasmuch as it transforms a story from the past into speech in the present. Poetry brings voice, value and an affective halo to what is said through rhythm. The main opposition in Meschonnic's poetics is not between poetry and ordinary language, but between poetry and a regime of language as word use, which diminishes the rhythmical continuity that makes discourse survive beyond the historical moment of its production. Poetry is sometimes opposed to narrative (*récit*) as understood by the French structuralist critics, as in the case of Esther, but at other times, to rhetoric,[15] ideology,[16] or even to poetry as sacred language.

It is important to remember that Meschonnic brings his initial intuition of the continuity between poetry and ordinary language to a theoretical stance, by adopting Wittgenstein's concept of language use, while criticizing its application to word and sentence use.[17] Meschonnic also takes issue with Wittgenstein's silence on the historicity of language use. The poetician considers that historicity is part of the language use in poetry, the main trait of poetic language being that it produces works that can speak in different contexts and to different forms of life. He was sensitive to the real power of transmission that poetic language holds, while trying to avoid explaining this power in terms of a universal language. The first duty of a poet and poetician is to denounce the 'ahistorical fallacy' of poetic language and instead to look for an explanation which preserves the historical character of this language. Rhythm is the solution; defined as the systemic organization of the subject in language, it can speak through the power of transformation of the subject across different political and social contexts.

The system of speech as the guarantee of historicity can appear to the reader accustomed to a systematic presentation as an axiom. Yet, from the perspective of his lifelong work, it is rather a working hypothesis that emerges from Meschonnic's own practice of writing and translation. A working hypothesis can never be offered a definitive demonstration. It can only be an angle of attack, so that various analyses of singular works transcend particularity and become state-ments on the relationship between poetic creation and its reception. Through the idea of rhythm, Meschonnic tried to answer questions that might have been considered metaphysical, therefore meaningless, by Wittgenstein: why certain artistic projects are continued by several individuals across time, while others are not? What makes certain texts, such as the Bible, meaningful even when the socio-political and theological context that produced them disappeared? How can a text have at the same time a literary, political and an ethical meaning? What makes him so close to Wittgenstein's investigations is his gesture to place poetry in continuity with ordinary language.

A poetics of the image: Jacques Roubaud

It is in dialogue with the photographic work of his wife, the photographer Alix Cleo Roubaud, an assiduous reader of Wittgenstein's *Tractatus* and *Philosophical Investigations*, that the French poet Jacques Roubaud begins to think of poetry in terms of the use of images. Chronologically, this dialogue coincides with the abandonment of what Roubaud called a *Project of Poetry* and of a novel supposed to accompany it, in the first pages of his six volume autobiographical *Le grand incendie de Londres*, written on the ruins of the Project. Before the 1980s, Roubaud theorized the difference between poetry and prose through generativist theories of rhythm (for example, Halle and Keyser[18]) that demonstrate the deep continuity between poetry and ordinary language. He argued that certain rhythms are naturally embedded (iambic pentameter is specific to the English language, the alexandrine to the French), a fact that ensures the survival and the stability of verbal material. Through this theory, Roubaud discovers a possible anthropological explanation of the role of poetry in human society as the laboratory of experimentation on the mnemonic function of language, already present in the accentual system of a particular language. On that occasion he coins his first anthropological definition of poetry: 'poetry is the memory of language'.

Because he finds rhythm in language (as *langue*) that excludes its creation by discourse (as Meschonnic has shown in his critique of Roubaud's theory of rhythm[19]) poetic rhythm is described by a formal mode, as a set of rules of combination and deviation from numerical patterns. A discourse in which no such rule can be unearthed is called prose. From within this theory of rhythm, since meaning is kept separate from prosody in the description, Roubaud will not be able to explain their relationship.

It is only through two theories of the image — Wittgenstein's *picture theory* and the *private language argument* on the one hand, and the *arts of memory* on the other — that Roubaud will articulate a theory where prosody is no longer separate from meaning. He calls it *formal meaning*, the meaningful form of a particular poem able to produce in its creator/reader an experiential pattern by transcending the particular mnemonically, similar to what Wittgenstein calls a *form of life*. This means that poetic form, unlike other linguistic forms, is produced as what Roubaud calls a *potential meaning*. For example, the *canso* is a rhythmical form that structures and potentially *encapsulates*[20] a specific form of erotic love, a complex experiential meaning that can be described, as in Wittgenstein's *Philosophical Investigations*, only by a minute analysis of the main 'statements' about love, considered the reminders of that complex form of life. Roubaud's book on the canso, *La fleur inverse*, is such a Wittgensteinien unfolding of the *formal meaning* of the *canso*, where the song, meters and rhyme structures organize mnemonically various statements about love, yielding a complex semantics of this word within the corpus of the troubadour poetry in twelfth-century Provence. In Roubaud's presentation, the selection of the reminders no longer seems arbitrary, as the selection of the statements about phenomena could have appeared in the *Philosophical Investigations*, because they belong to a tradition distilled mnemonically by centuries of poetry reading.

For Roubaud, the mnemonic distillation is further explained by a certain type of poetic image that he calls *image-poésie*, recalling Mallarmé's 'image rhythms'.[21] This is a specific *memory image* enriched or induced by the reading-writing of specific poems. Prose brings about another type of image, which he calls *piction*, and which functions like a photograph or a diagram, in that the individual memory cannot recognize this image as being its own while reading about it. *Piction* is a mot-valise that combines the words 'fiction' and 'picture,' an image that is fictive in relation to the real.

The *memory image*, as well as the *image-poésie*, are — through the movement of memory that includes them — in direct relationship to the world, being 'the change in me induced by something in the world'.[22] Roubaud's radical difference between *image-poésie* and *piction* is most mysterious to his readers. In order fully to grasp this difference, I would like to trace it back to its source, which is Wittgenstein's theory of the image.

After Alix's premature death (in 1983), engaging with Wittgenstein's entire life work was, for Roubaud, a means of preserving a way of life invented by the couple in a dialogue between poetry, photography and philosophy. Wittgenstein's theory of the image concerns not what can be *seen* of the world, but what can be *said* about the world. The *Investigations* discourage the reader from entering the dark forest of philosophical claims about the 'ineffable' and 'invisible' nature of the soul and of its constituents (sensation, mental representation, thoughts, pain). In the *Blue and Brown Books*, Wittgenstein shows that when crossing the line between what can be said and what cannot be said, one changes an active image that speaks into an idle image (*image oisive, müßiges Bild*), which only seems to speak. Sentences like 'only I can know whether I am really in pain; another person can only surmise it' are grammatical, not empirical. This means that the word 'pain' has to be associated with such invisibility, this being its very meaning in language. Thereby, what seems to be an empirical given — the invisibility of pain — is founded by language use alone. All claims of invisibility (of sensation, of pain) are sentences that are misused and abused, which go beyond 'what can be said' about the world. When dismissing such mistakes and claims of invisibility, Wittgenstein develops a theory of the *idle image*, which he compares with a painting that a worker would contemplate instead of using it to implement something.[23]

The idle image is rigid in that it is set apart from the real movement of thought and thus from a change in the real world through language (a way of life). The active image does always produce a movement and a change in the world. It is through this movement that it speaks. Wittgenstein shows that the main source of idle images is the fact that people use language games about objects in the world in order to express sentiments, sensations and emotions.

It is in relation to these multiple oppositions — inner/outer; idle/active; expressive/descriptive — that Roubaud will elaborate his theory of the poetic image and formal meaning. It is important to remember that unlike Meschonnic, Roubaud's remarks on Wittgenstein are part of his unusual autobiographical prose in which they function as part of a narrative 'explanation' of the genesis and ethical principles that informed his own poetry, on the background of a life split into a before and an after Alix's death and the abandonment of his 'Project of poetry', a life organized symbolically (grammatically), as in Dante's *Vita Nuova*.

Yet, why should the active image be associated with poetry, and the idle image with narrative? This association means that somehow poetry is closer to ordinary language, while narrative is closer to the mistaken linguistic usages of philosophers. From the perspective of 'what can be said' about the world, this claim becomes intuitive in the following manner. The way in which we can check if something can be said about the world is for Wittgenstein a matter of memory, more specifically, of reminders. One has to remember the ways in which one uses language. This means that one has to remember the statements, the situations in which they are uttered, and the 'positions' of the actors who take part in that situation. This fits, almost too well, Roubaud's own poetic principle, that *poetry is the memory of language*. In this sense, it is poetry that will be able to take up the role that Wittgenstein assigns to philosophical investigation, while it is the domain of traditional autobiographical narrative to make irresponsible claims about the creative mind understood as a treasure of 'inner images' to be described.

A poem learned by heart induces and organizes one's memory, without denoting real objects in the world. The poems refer to a mnemonic configuration *indirectly*, metaphorically, elliptically, and most important *rhythmically*. In *La boucle* ('The Loop') the second volume of his autobiographical prose, Roubaud explains that a poem by the medieval poet Rimbaut d'Aurenga that begins 'an resplan la flors enversa ('Now the flower shines, perverse') ' has been associated with a series of old childhood memories during the war, that crystallize around one central memory image: he is in his room in Carcassone before a window covered by ice flowers. The narrative will unveil that the medieval poem read and learned by heart later in his life functioned as a trigger ('un effecteur de mémoire') of this cloud of memory images, configured by poetic rumination. The poem functions thus as the expressive reminder of this cloud of experience. Similar to the use of psychological sentences in Wittgenstein's *Remarks on the Philosophy of Psychology*, the poem does not 'designate' objects in the world or states of mind. The metaphoric 'indirection' preserves the movement and freshness of the plastic configuration of experience as what Wittgenstein often calls the 'surrounding' of statements, and thus allows for a new poem, with new words, and new rhythms, be written on the basis of this same configuration. For example, Roubaud wrote an 'elastic sonnet' published in 1967, 'Signe d'appartenance',[24] based on the experience already crystallized by Aurenga's canso. Its form recalls Aurenga's poem, which uses different formal constraints and tropes, in the same way that historically the sonnet as formal meaning is the memory of the canso.

When language refers in a direct descriptive manner to the experience of the ice flower, the writer obtains a *piction* that narrates and describes it, in 'La Boucle'.[25] A *piction* is an image saturated by language, inasmuch as nothing remains 'outside' direct designation within a protocol of descriptive determination. It is similar to the image in the space defined by the *Tractatus*: (2.1511) 'That is how a picture is attached to reality; it reaches right out to it. (2.1512) It is laid against reality like a measure. (2.15121)- Only the end-points of the graduating lines actually touch the object that is to be measured'. Thus, Roubaud compares the *piction* to a photograph in words, in that, like in a photograph, there is no part of the image that can move or change after the description is over. The description thus exhausts the image, in both senses: it wears it out as it fully describes it.[26] Roubaud thus defines a poetics where experience exceeds what is written down on the page. By the difference between *images-poésie* and *pictions*, he wants to say that each poem that stays before our eyes has been an experience that 'exceeds, obviously, what I retained to write down'.[27] This excess is encapsulated by metaphoric–rhythmic encapsulation of experience (in its main and meaningful lines) by poetic rumination.

In his poetry written after the death of his wife, and after the abandonment of the *Projet de poésie*, Roubaud will reject this metaphorical excess by attempting to invent a regime of the poetic rule that allows the reader to construct the meaning of what is written about a world from the rhythmical syncope of discourse alone. This resembles in all aspects Meschonnic's conception of rhythm as subject-formation, yet unlike Meschonnic, Roubaud will work out a non-dialectical theory of the subject that he found in Wittgenstein. This new regime of the rule is inspired by the theory of language games in which people explore together a shared memory of language and, thus, resist the temptation of using inner images to justify the functioning of language. Roubaud invents a new word to describe this new function of the rule — *biipsism* — which is neither the solipsist mind, nor the collective and habitual activity, but *a rule for two people*. Roubaud describes this existence of the *biipsist rule*, in a poem entitled 'Une logique', published in the volume of elegies composed after the death of his wife:

> Une sorte de logique pour laquelle tu aurais construit
> un sens moi une syntaxe, un modèle, des calculs
> Le monde d'un seul, mais qui aurait été deux : pas un
> solipsisme, un *biipsisme*
> Le nombre un, mais comme bougé dans le miroir, dans
> deux miroirs se faisant face
>
> (A kind of logic for which you would have built
> a meaning me, a syntax, a model, calculations
> The world of one alone, but one who would have been two: not a
> solipsism, a *biipsism*.
> The number one, but as if moved in a mirror,
> two mirrors facing one another)[28]

The theory of *biipsism* plays in Roubaud the same role that dialectics plays in Meschonnic. It is a theory of the subject able to account for the articulation of the creative and the receptive process as well as the historicity of poetic language present in its rhythmical form. The theory of *biipsism* originates in the experience of the death of the privileged reader of his poetry, Alix. Roubaud's theory of historicity is thus essentially elegiac. While Meschonnic wanted his dialectics of the reading/writing of poetry to overcome the opposition between life and death, optimism and pessimism, Roubaud puts forward a fundamentally non-dialectical understanding of the subject, who as in Wittgenstein is essentially powerless regarding the world of facts.[29] By replacing *solipsism* with *biipsism* he makes a statement about the fundamental historicity of poetic language, which is in this sense different from the language used to describe a world of objects, predicated by Wittgenstein on the instantaneous coincidence, not difference of two minds. In the preface to the *Tractatus*, Wittgenstein had written: 'Perhaps this book will be understood only by someone who has himself already had the thoughts that are expressed in it — or at least similar thoughts' (*TLP*, 'Preface', 3). 'Une logique' claims that poetry springs from a fundamental difference between two minds, and across a distance that cannot be measured and which is essentially temporal. The subject as two mirrors that face each other replaces the Tractarian analogy between the subject and the eye at the limit of one's visual field, while the certainty of the Tractarian future anterior — 'will already have thought' — switches to a conditional past tense (*tu aurais construit*) that emphasizes its fundamental rarity in the world. Poetry is a language-use that is fundamentally a meditation on death that informs its power of transmission. The lyrical subject has to face a world that does no longer contain a real you, either in the form of a concrete reader of poetry that will give meaning to poetic words, or in the form of an artistic community of composers of poems. Thus, while maintaining the lines in which Wittgenstein defines the subject, Roubaud explicitly takes issue with the statements in the *Tractatus* or his later philosophy that refuse to think of death in relation to the uses of language.

Here are two examples of such poetic refutation, from the collection *Quelque chose noir*. First, the poem 'Mort' (*QCN*, 66) combines a previous text written by Roubaud about the form of the tale (*conte*),[30] with a long quotation coming from Alix's diary in which she speaks of her own death by referring to the famous passage at the end of the *Tractatus*. Roubaud's theory of the tale is much indebted to Wittgenstein's *Tractatus*. The power of language to say something true to everyone who listens is transferred by Roubaud from the domain of logic to that of the tale.[31] The death of the beloved has replaced the tale (taken as a utopia of the subject in language); the death no longer says anything, but does nevertheless speak to anyone who listens. Death is thus something striking and obvious, which affirms the coincidence between the still images from Alix's photographs that stage her own death, the words in her diary and the world. Death had appeared at the end of the *Tractatus*, as something that cannot be an event in the world (6.4311: *Ereignis des Lebens*). This distinction between the world of facts and the whole world as elegiac feeling (here 'pain') is marked by Roubaud by the distinction between saying and speaking ('dire' and 'parler'). In the text on the tale, the verb was not 'parle vrai,' but 'dire vrai.' 'Dire' is what can be said. 'Parler' is what speaks even if nothing is said, or something beyond what is said; as in the expression 'ceci me parle, cela non' ('this speaks to me. Not this').

The most systematic references to Wittgenstein in *Quelque chose noir* are to the late text, *On Certainty*. This book takes as a point of departure several sentences analysed by G. E. Moore, in order to refute sceptical positions such as the inexistence of the world. Three such sentences are taken into Wittgenstein's book: the main sentence is 'here is one hand'; the second sentence is: 'the earth had existed also for many years before my body was born'; and the third 'I know that is a tree'. The same sentences appear as key images in Roubaud's volume of poetry: the hand is the image of death; the earth that has existed before I was born is transformed into the earth that remains after 'your' death; and 'I know that is a tree' becomes the allegorical affirmation of memory. All these three images link a world of pain (the earth after the beloved's death), with images void of a world (her hand), by means of memory (the tree). The imagery of the volume spells out the apotheosis of the beloved, a figure with which the pastoral elegy of Romantic and Victorian poetry ends its lamentation, by assimilating in the poem two language games that defined the beloved: the description of photographs and the argumentation on language.

I will take as the example of refutation of *On Certainty* the poem on the 'hand', which contains the most violent image of the dead woman, repeated as something that cannot be linked to anything else:

> Il y avait du sang sous ta peau   dans ta main
> tombé au bout des doigts   je ne le voyais pas humain.
> Cette image se présente pour la millième fois   à neuf
> avec la même violence   elle ne peut pas ne pas se
> répéter indéfiniment   une nouvelle génération de mes
> cellules   si temps il y a   trouvera cette duplication
> onéreuse ces tirages photographiques internes   je n'ai
> pas le choix   maintenant. (*QCN*, 11)

> (There was blood under your skin   in your hand
> fallen at the end of your fingers   I didn't see it as human.
> This image presents itself for the thousandth time new
> with the same violence   it cannot not
> repeat itself indefinitely   another generation of my
> cells   if there is time   will find this duplication
> arduous   these prints internal photographs   I have
> no choice   now.)

This image reappears constantly in the volume, until it is absorbed into the light of the setting sun in the last poem, reminding the reader of apotheosis in traditional elegy: the open evening sky that receives the soul of the deceased. The photograph-like reproduction of the hand affirms a rigid image that shatters the mind, so that it cannot recite, nor communicate, nor sing. Time itself seems broken like an overworked engine caught in a disastrous repetition. The memorable first sentence from Wittgenstein's text: 'if you do know that here is one hand, we'll grant you all the rest' is twisted in the poetic text. The ostensive certainty is emptied of its very gesture. A hand devoid of gesture, a lifeless hand drooping out of the bed, a lifeless remainder, not a reminder: 'je savais qu'il y avait là une main. Qui m'accorderait désormais tout le reste?' (*QCN*, 32: 'I knew that there was a hand there. Who would grant me, henceforth, all the rest'). There is nevertheless a hand as gesture in the poem, not seen, nor shown, although present in the art of memory that the volume enacts. This is the 'mnemonic hand' used as a technique of memorization in *Quelque chose noir*. In the nine strophes of each poem, one can detect nine places (*loci*) on the hand, where the words are attached; the mnemonic hand is the same, the images and words change. The poet thus triggers the dynamics between the free imagination of the reader and the poem, which in Meschonnic was mediated by rhythm.

For Meschonnic and Roubaud, Wittgenstein is a primary thinker of the subject in language, an alternative voice to the mainstream methods of analysis dominated, in particular, by the rejection of the subject by structuralist of post-structuralist philosophers. For these poets, Wittgenstein is the philosopher who thinks of the relationship between language and lived experience in a new way, and at the same time in more subtle terms than the aesthetic analysis and upfront political commitment of the new avant-gardes of their time. In short, Wittgenstein's critique of all theories that depart from real linguistic practice offers these poets a new springboard from where to think of the extraordinary role that poetry can play in society if poetry is in contact with the linguistic practices of ordinary language.

Yet, their own appropriation of Wittgenstein is fundamentally different, dependent on their specific treatment of the relationship between language and death. For Meschonnic poetic language, because of its vocation to transform the subject through discourse, overcomes death, while it intertwines dialectically various acts of writing and reading, creative impulses and receptive willingness. For

Roubaud, poetic language alone is able to give linguistic expression to death, whereas the subject in language is suspended in the margins of a linguistic community. Poetry can in this way be conceived as a meditation on death that springs from the ultimate fissure between the act of writing and the act of reading in the contemporary world. It thus reveals the elegiac condition of poetry today: the lyrical subject exists in a world that no longer contains any ascertained addressee, either in the form of a community readers, or of poets, composers, that would share a memory shaped by the rumination of poems.

NOTES

1 Henri Meschonnic, *Pour la poétique V. La poésie sans réponse* (Paris: Gallimard, 1978), 37–61.

2 Meschonnic, *Pour la poétique*, V, 37.

3 Meschonnic, *Pour la poétique*, II (Paris: Gallimard, 1973), 153.

4 All translations from the *Tractatus* from Ludwig Wittgenstein, *Tractatus Logico-Philosophicus*, translated by D.F. Pears and B.F. McGuiness (London: Routledge, 1991), henceforward *TLP*, followed by the number of the proposition.

5 Meschonnic is particularly critical of the Tel Quel movement for having unduly formalized and politicized a practice that is essentially 'sans modèle'. See *Pour la poétique* II, chapter 'Pratique et théorie de « Tel Quel »', 84–138.

6 Ludwig Wittgenstein, *Philosophical Investigations*, translated by G.E.M. Anscombe, 3rd edition (Oxford : Oxford University Press, 2001), §144. Henceforward *PI*.

7 Christiane Chauviré, *L'Immanence de l'ego* (Paris: PUF, 2009), 79.

8 Alain Badiou, *L'Antiphilosophie de Wittgenstein* (Caen: Nous, 2009) 47.

9 Henri Meschonnic, *Critique du rythme : Anthropologie historique du langage* (Paris: Verdier, 1982); *Politique du rythme, politique du sujet* (Paris: Verdier, 1995).

10 Henri Meschonnic, 'Le signe et l'écriture dans le sacré', in *Le signe et le poème* (Paris: Gallimard, 1975).

11 Emile Benveniste, 'Les relations de temps dans le verbe français', *Problèmes de linguistique générale* (Paris: Gallimard, 1966), 238.

12 The distinction between story and discourse has played an important role in narratology. As a theory of reading, structuralism had to separate the imaginary from the empirical, concretely the real reader from the ideal reader and the author from the narrator.

13 Henri Meschonnic, *Cinq Rouleaux* (Paris: Gallimard, 1970), 14, henceforward *CR*.

14   See, in particular, Meschonnic's comments on the *Esther* translation in *CR*, 191.

15   Mostly in his *Pour la poétique I* (Paris: Gallimard, 1970) and his *Critique du rythme*, especially 'Critique, historicité de la théorie', 'Le rythme sans mesure' and 'Situations du rythme'.

16   Mostly developed in *Politique du rythme* and *Modernité, modernité* (Paris: Verdier, 1988).

17   Meschonnic, *Cinq Rouleaux*, 13.

18   See for example Morris Halle and Samuel Jay Keyser, 'Chaucer and the Study of Prosody', *College English* 28 (1966), 187–219: a seminal article.

19   Henri Meschonnic, *Critique du rythme*, the chapter entitled 'le même est le même est le même'. Here he takes issue with Roubaud's book on the history of the alexandrine in French: *La Vieillesse d'Alexandre*.

20   Jacques Roubaud, *Poésie* (Paris: Seuil, 2000), 14.

21   Stéphane Mallarmé, *Oeuvres Complètes* (Paris: Gallimard, Bibliothèque de la Pléiade, 1998), 1050.

22   Jacques Roubaud, *La Boucle* (Paris: Seuil, 1993), 252.

23   Wittgenstein, *PI*, §291.

24   Jacques Roubaud, ∈ (Paris: Gallimard, 1967), 22–3.

25   Jacques Roubaud, *La Boucle*, 11.

26   The idea of a language that wears out comes from another tradition that Roubaud cherishes — the arts of memory — which makes the distinction between the active (*imagines agentes*) and idle images in terms of active as opposed to a worn-out image. This is the tradition of the arts of memory that he discovers in Francis Yates's *Arts of Memory*.

27   Jacques Roubaud, *La bibliothèque de Warburg* (Paris: Seuil, 2002), 144.

28   Jacques Roubaud, *Quelque chose noir* (Paris: Gallimard, 1986), 50–1. Translations by James Helgeson, henceforward *QCN*.

29   As in the *TLP*, 6.373: 'The world is independent of my will', and its present manifest only as the limit of the world' (5.632) 'The subject does not belong to the world, but is the limit of the world'.

30   Jacques Roubaud, 'Poésie, mémoire, nombre, temps, rythme, contrainte, forme, etc.: Remarques', *Mezura* 35 (1995), 20.

31   Explicit references to both Wittgenstein's works and their concepts appear in 'Poésie, mémoire...' in *Mezura* 35, remarks G and H.

Notes on Contributors

Jacques Bouveresse is Professor Emeritus at the Collège de France, where he held the chair of philosophy of language and epistemology from 1995 to 2010. Long the preeminent French specialist on Wittgenstein, he has written additionally on a number of subjects including Robert Musil, Karl Kraus, analytic philosophy, philosophy of science, epistemology and philosophy of mathematics.

Reidar Due is University Lecturer in European Cinema and Fellow in French at Magdalen College, Oxford. His research interests are film theory, semiotics, philosophical aesthetics and the history of French philosophy. He is a specialist of the thought of Gilles Deleuze, on which he has published a monograph (Cambridge: Polity, 2006) and edited a collection of articles.

Garry L. Hagberg is James H. Ottaway Professor of Philosophy and Aesthetics at Bard College, and has in recent years also held a Chair in the School of Philosophy at the University of East Anglia. Author of numerous papers at the intersection of aesthetics and the philosophy of language, his books include *Meaning and Interpretation: Wittgenstein, Henry James, and Literary Knowledge*, and *Art as Language: Wittgenstein, Meaning, and Aesthetic Theory*; his *Describing Ourselves: Wittgenstein and Autobiographical Consciousness* appeared with Oxford University Press in 2008. An edited collection, *Art and Ethical Criticism*, recently appeared with Blackwell, and he is co-editor of *The Blackwell Companion to the Philosophy of Literature* (2010) and editor of the journal *Philosophy and Literature*.

Jonathan Havercroft is Assistant Professor of Political Science at the University of Oklahoma. He specializes in political theory, with a primary focus on the historical transformation of sovereignty in political philosophy from the seventeenth century to the present.

Paragraph 34.3 (2011): 441–442
DOI: 10.3366/para.2011.0035
© Edinburgh University Press
www.eupjournals.com/para

He is the author of *Captives of Sovereignty* (Cambridge: Cambridge University Press, 2011).

James Helgeson teaches at the University of Nottingham. He was formerly Associate Professor of French at Columbia University in New York and Assistant Lecturer at Cambridge. He has published extensively on early modern literature and thought as well as on literary theory and its intersections with philosophy. His second book, *The Lying Mirror: the First Person Stance and Sixteenth-Century Writing* (Geneva: Droz, 2011) is forthcoming this autumn.

Alison James is Assistant Professor of French at the University of Chicago. She specializes in modern and contemporary French literature, in particular the Oulipo group, experimental poetry and prose, the connections between literature and philosophy, and representations of the everyday. Her book *Constraining Chance: Georges Perec and the Oulipo* was published by Northwestern University Press (2009). She has published extensively on contemporary literary and philosophical topics.

Sandra Laugier is Professor of Philosophy at the University of Paris-I Panthéon-Sorbonne. She has written important work on Wittgenstein, Austin and moral philosophy and has also been instrumental in the reception of several aspects of American philosophy in France, in particular the work of W.V.O. Quine, Cora Diamond and Stanley Cavell. Among other works, she is the author of a recent study on Wittgenstein: *Wittgenstein, le sens de l'usage* (Paris: Vrin, 2009).

Maria Rusanda Muresan is a post-doctoral researcher at the Ecole Normale Supérieure (rue d'Ulm) in Paris. She has written extensively on philosophy and poetics in France. Her work has concentrated on the intersection in recent poetics of two fields of enquiry: the French literary reception of Wittgenstein and post-war Anglo-American philosophy of language, and the relation between poetry and memory in Jacques Roubaud and other contemporary poets. She has a book forthcoming on these subjects from Klincksieck.

Index:

Paragraph 34 (2011)

34.2 *Claude Imbert in Perspective: Creation, Cognition and Modern Experience*, edited by Adriana Bontea and Boris Wiseman

34.3 *Wittgenstein, Theory, Literature*, edited by James Helgeson

LUCY BELL
Articulations of the Real: from Lacan to Badiou   **34:1**, 105–120

ADRIANA BONTEA
Conceptual Invention   **34:2**, 217–232

ADRIANA BONTEA AND BORIS WISEMAN
Introduction   **34:2**, 155–157

JACQUES BOUVERESSE
Wittgenstein, von Wright and the Myth of Progress   **34:3**, 301–321

RACHEL BOWLBY
'Half Art': Baudelaire's *Le Peintre de la vie moderne*   **34:1**, 1–11

CÜNEYT ÇAKIRLAR
Masculinity, Scatology, Mooning and the Queer/able Art of Gilbert & George: On the Visual Discourse of Male Ejaculation and Anal Penetration   **34:1**, 86–104

PENELOPE DEUTSCHER
Manière du départ: Beauvoir, Merleau-Ponty and Lévi-Strauss Take their Leave   **34:2**, 233–243

SOULEYMANE BACHIR DIAGNE
From the Tower of Babel to the Ladder of Jacob: Claude Imbert Reading Merleau-Ponty   **34:2**, 244–256

SUZANNE DOW
Beckett's Humour, from an Ethics of Finitude to
an Ethics of the Real   **34:1**, 121–136

REIDAR A. DUE
At the Margins of Sense: The Function of Paradox in
Deleuze and Wittgenstein   **34:3**, 358–370

GARRY L. HAGBERG
Wittgenstein's *Philosophical Investigations*, Linguistic
Meaning and Music   **34:3**, 388–405

JAIME HANNEKEN
Scandal, Choice and the Economy of Minority
Literature   **34:1**, 48–65

JONATHAN HAVERCROFT
Skinner, Wittgenstein and Historical Method   **34:3**, 371–387

JAMES HELGESON
Introduction   **34:3**, 287–300

JAMES HELGESON
What Cannot Be Said: Notes on Early French
Wittgenstein Reception   **34:3**, 338–357

CLAUDE IMBERT
Maurice Merleau-Ponty   **34:2**, 167–186

CLAUDE IMBERT
Manet, Effects of Black   **34:2**, 187–198

ALISON JAMES
The Surrealism of the Habitual: From Poetic
Language to the Prose of Life   **34:3**, 406–422

JEAN KHALFA
Jean Cavaillès on the Effectiveness of Symbolic
Thought   **34:2**, 257–265

FRÉDÉRIC KECK

The Ruins of Participation: Claude Imbert's
Anthropology of Logic   **34:2**, 266–278

SANDRA LAUGIER

Pierre Hadot as a Reader of Wittgenstein   **34:3**, 322–337

MARIA RUSANDA MURESAN

Wittgenstein in Recent French Poetics: Henri
Meschonnic and Jacques Roubaud   **34:3**, 423–440

SANJA PEROVIC

The Intelligible as a New World? Wikipedia versus the
Eighteenth-Century *Encyclopédie*   **34:1**, 12–29

CHRISTOPHER PETERSON

Slavery's Bestiary: Joel Chandler Harris's
Uncle Remus Tales   **34:1**, 30–47

KATHERINE SHINGLER

Perceiving Text and Image in Apollinaire's
Calligrammes   **34:1**, 66–85

BORIS WISEMAN

Kaleidoscope   **34:2**, 199–216

SIMON MORGAN WORTHAM

Infant Criticism: Agamben's Potential   **34:1**, 137–151

An Interview with Claude Imbert   **34:2**, 158–166

Select Bibliography of Works by Claude Imbert   **34:2**, 279–282

The Irish Journal of French Studies

(Les Cahiers de l'ADEFFI)

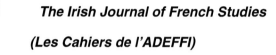

EDITORIAL BOARD

General Editor, Johnnie Gratton **grattonj@tcd.ie**

Co-Editors, Michael Brophy, Jane Conroy and Emer O'Beirne

La revue annuelle de l'Association des Etudes Françaises et Francophones d'Irlande, *The Irish Journal of French Studies* (Les Cahiers de l'Adeffi), est une revue internationale qui publie des articles en français, en anglais ou en irlandais sur des sujets appartenant aux domaines des cultures et sociétés françaises et francophones. Si vous désirez proposer un article, veuillez en envoyer trois copies. Les articles ne doivent normalement ni dépasser les 6000 mots ni avoir été soumis à d'autre publication. Après acceptation, Les Cahiers en détiennent les droits exclusifs.

The Irish Journal of French Studies is an annual international refereed journal published by the *Association des Etudes Françaises et Francophones d'Irlande*. Articles in English, French or Irish are welcomed on any aspect of research in the area of French and Francophone culture and society, on condition that they have not been submitted to another journal and that the *IJFrS* has exclusive rights to publication. They should not normally exceed 6000 words. If you wish to propose an article, please send two hard copies.

Tous articles, lettres et ouvrages doivent parvenir à Professeur Johnnie Gratton; Department of French, Trinity College Dublin, Dublin 2. All correspondence and books for review should be addressed to Professor Johnnie Gratton; Department of French, Trinity College Dublin, Dublin 2.

symplokē

a journal for the intermingling of literary, cultural and theoretical scholarship

editor-in-chief
Jeffrey R. Di Leo

associate editor
Ian Buchanan

advisory board
Charles Altieri
Michael Bérubé
Ronald Bogue
Matei Calinescu
Edward Casey
Stanley Corngold
Lennard Davis
Robert Con Davis
Henry Giroux
Karen Hanson
Phillip Brian Harper
Peter C. Herman
Candace Lang
Vincent B. Leitch
Paisley Livingston
Donald Marshall
Christian Moraru
Jeffrey Nealon
Marjorie Perloff
Mark Poster
Gerald Prince
Joseph Ricapito
Robert Scholes
Alan Schrift
Tobin Siebers
Hugh Silverman
John H. Smith
Paul M. Smith
James Sosnoski
Henry Sussman
Mark Taylor
S. Tötösy de Zepetnek
Joel Weinsheimer
Jeffrey Williams

submissions
Editor, symplokē
School of Arts & Sciences
University of Houston-Victoria
Victoria, TX 77901-5731
email editor@symploke.org

subscriptions
University of Nebraska Press
1111 Lincoln Mall
Lincoln, NE 68588-0630

www.symploke.org

symplokē is a comparative theory and literature journal. Our aim is to provide an arena for critical exchange between established and emerging voices in the field. We support new and developing notions of comparative literature, and are committed to interdisciplinary studies, intellectual pluralism, and open discussion. We are particularly interested in scholarship on the interrelations among philosophy, literature, culture criticism and intellectual history, though will consider articles on any aspect of the intermingling of discourses and disciplines.

forthcoming issues
EMOTIONS ✤ HUNGER

past issues
GAMING AND THEORY ✤ ANONYMITY
CINEMA WITHOUT BORDERS ✤ DISCOURAGEMENT
COLLEGIALITY ✤   FICTION'S PRESENT
PRACTICING DELEUZE AND GUATTARI
ANTHOLOGIES ✤ SITES OF PEDAGOGY
RHETORIC & THE HUMAN SCIENCES

some past & future contributors
Michael Apple on doing critical educational work
Peter Baker on deconstruction and violence
Tom Conley on border incidence
Ronald Bogue on minor literature
Frederick Buell on globalization and environmentalism
Matei Calinescu on modernity and modernization
Peter Caws on sophistry and postmodernity
Claire Colebrook on happiness, theoria, and everyday life
David Damrosch on world literature anthologies
Samuel R. Delany on fiction's present
Elizabeth Ellsworth on pedagogy and the holocaust museum
Brian Evenson on fiction and philosophy
Caryl Emerson on berlin, bakhtin and relativism
John Frow on terror and cultural studies
Elizabeth Grosz on the future in deleuze
Alphonso Lingis on bestiality
Cris Mazza on postfeminist literature
John Mowitt on queer resistance
David Palumbo-Liu on asian america and the imaginary
Marjorie Perloff on poetry and affiliation
Steven Shaviro on the sublime
David Shumway on marxism without revolution
John Smith on queering the will
William V. Spanos on humanism after 9/11
J. Hillis Miller on boundaries in toni morrison
Jeffrey Williams on the posttheory generation
Ewa Ziarek on foucault's ethics

please enter my one-year subscription (two issues) to *symplokē*
❑ Individuals: $20   ❑ Institutions: $40   Add $15 for subscriptions outside the U.S.

Name

Address   Apt.

City   State   Zip

2000 CELJ PHOENIX AWARD FOR SIGNIFICANT EDITORIAL ACHIEVEMENT

PRODUCED AND DISTRIBUTED IN ASSOCIATION WITH THE UNIVERSITY OF NEBRASKA PRESS